WALKING IN THE ALGARVE

About the Author

Julie Statham has lived in the Algarve since 1998, moving there from France where she was an active walk leader for four years. Originally from the UK she has an Earth Sciences degree from the Open University and a degree and doctorate in Geology from Bristol University; today she is especially interested in conservation and environmental protection.

Since moving to the Algarve walking has become her life. She now runs her own company – Portugal Walks – which offers walking holidays throughout the country. Julie is passionate about the potential of the Algarve for walking, and is constantly seeking new paths and trails – 'it's an obsession'. She also runs a walking club for residents which meets every fortnight and raises money for charity. To relax Julie likes to sample good Portuguese wine – preferably red!

CONTENTS

Map Key

`·-·---`	walk route (various colours)
road symbol	road
N124	road numbers
habitation symbol	habitation
▲	summit
dam symbol	dam
lake symbol	sea/lake/tarn
river symbol	river
●	start/finish of walk
◉	city/town
◦	village
□	house/building
fort symbol	fort
•	spot height
↗	pointer to places off map

Contour colour key

	600-700m
	500-600m
	400-500m
	300-400m
	200-300m
	100-200m
	0-100m

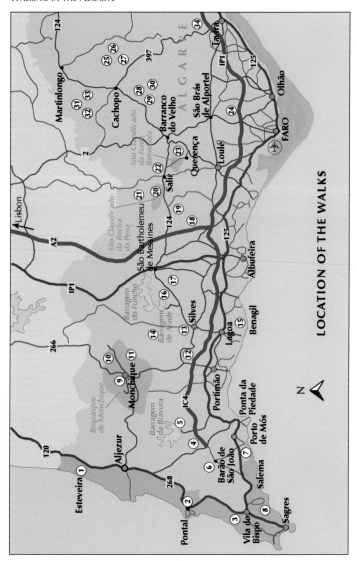

LOCATION OF THE WALKS

PREFACE TO THE SECOND EDITION

The first edition of this guide, *Walking in the Algarve* by the late June Parker, was the first walking guide to the area, and quickly became an essential accessory for all those who enjoyed getting out and exploring the Algarve on foot. June researched the walks in the early 1990s, but since that time much of the area has undergone an extensive transformation not only in terms of new building developments but also the addition of an extensive new road system. These changes, coupled with the deterioration of many tracks and paths, meant that a complete overhaul of the guide was necessary. Where possible I have included some of June's original walks but I have also researched new ones; together these reflect the varied nature of the area.

I am deeply indebted to Elizabeth Shaper, Peter and Ann Statham, and Silvia Smeman, who have helped me find new tracks and paths and have tried and tested many of the new walks. This book is dedicated to them, and to all those who have come walking regularly with me over the past seven years.

Julie Statham, 2005

Through the Esteveira nature reserve (Walk 1)

INTRODUCTION

The area of southern Portugal known as the Algarve has been the destination for winter-sun-seekers for many years. Although bordered by the Atlantic Ocean to both the south and west it is warmed by the Gulf Stream and experiences a Mediterranean climate with hot, dry summers and mild, sunny winters. The oft-quoted statistic – that the Algarve receives an average of 300 days sunshine a year – is true.

For many years the Algarve was not considered a 'real' walking destination, but rather the domain of golfers in winter and sun-worshippers during the summer months, but that opinion is rapidly changing.

An increasing number of people, drawn to the area by low-cost flights, are beginning to realise that there is far more to this area than first meets the eye. Besides the spectacular and dramatic coastline – much of which still remains unspoilt – there is a huge interior that most tourists never visit. Here there is a rich variety of landscape – from the mountains of the Serra to rolling foothills interspersed with dramatic limestone escarpments. With the changes in scenery come variations in the local flora and fauna, which combine to make walking here so very interesting. In addition there are still many villages that see very few – if any – tourists, places where the mule and plough still work the land and where laundry is done by hand at the local wash-house.

Porto do Mos in the distance (Walk 7)

It is fair to say that parts of the coastline were, in the past, overwhelmed by building developments to satisfy tourist demand, and some small fishing villages became large resorts almost overnight. That unrestricted growth has now been controlled, and steps have been taken to protect areas of natural beauty. All of the western Atlantic coastline – where some of the best coastal walking can be found – is now included in the Cape St Vincent Natural Park, and nature reserves have been created along the coast near Castro Marim and Faro to help preserve important wetland areas. The same is true for unique inland sites such as the limestone escarpment of Rocha de Pena, the Fonte de Benemola near Querença, and the banks of the Rio Guadiana on the Spanish border.

The distribution of walks in this guide offers a good mix of coastal, mountain and inland scenery. The majority can be tackled by anyone of average fitness, and the grading used is based on the amount of climbing involved: an easy walk is a flat walk suitable for all the family, whereas a difficult walk (there are very few) would involve a number of fairly steep ascents and descents.

The walks are, for the most part, well away from the main tourist developments, and because public transport is poor you will need a car to get to the start of most routes. Once away from the coast there are few facilities such as cafes and

restaurants, so if you are choosing one of the longer walks do make sure you take refreshments with you, including plenty of water.

The majority of the walks are located to the north and west of Faro, and there are very few close to the Spanish border. This is because the coast is a series of sand flats which do not lend themselves to good walking, while inland the rolling hills have very poor access. The best walking is found a good 30 miles or so from the coast around Cachopo, and these are included in this guide.

WHEN TO GO

The Algarve has one of the best climates in Europe, with an average annual temperature of 17°C. The summers are long, hot and dry, and cloudless blue skies can be guaranteed day after day. August, with a maximum average of 27.5°C, is not a suitable month for walking unless you are prepared to go out as the sun is rising!

The ideal months for walking are late September through to early June. Spring is particularly lovely: in January and February millions of almond trees come into flower, producing beautiful blossoms in profusion before the leaves appear, so that whole hillsides have a pink and white glow. The spring flowers also begin to appear and are in full bloom during March and April, when orange blossom fills the air with a heady fragrant scent.

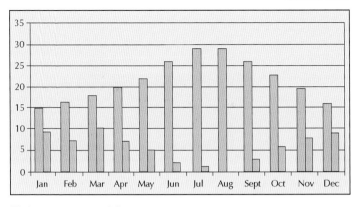

■ Average temperature (°C)

■ Average number of rainy days

First-time visitors should also be aware that there is a distinct temperature gradient between east and west. It is noticeably cooler in the west; often, while the southern coastline is experiencing blue skies and hot sunshine, the cliffs and beaches along the western Atlantic can be enveloped in dense, chilling sea fog. The western Algarve is also much windier, and from Portimão westwards the region is commonly known as 'Barlavento' (the windward side).

Rainfall is unpredictable, except for its absence during the summer months. Most of the annual rain occurs between October and May, but there is no knowing when. The rain usually comes from frontal systems that pass over the region from west to east and is likely to be torrential, usually clearing up in a matter of hours.

GETTING THERE

Flying to the Algarve from the United Kingdom has never been easier. British Airways (www.ba.com) and TAP (www.tap-airportugal.co.uk) have daily scheduled flights to Faro airport from London, and Monarch from London and Manchester (www.flymonarch.com). The low-cost airline EasyJet (www.easyjet.com) flies daily to Faro from Stansted, Luton, Gatwick and Bristol. Other low-cost airlines are beginning to offer flights from many regional airports so it is worth checking with your preferred airport.

It is also possible to fly into Lisbon with both British Airways and TAP and then take the train down to the Algarve; the journey takes about 3 hours. The train service is excellent; full details of all trains can be found on the website www.cp.pt.

13

Local transport, Carrapateira (Walk 2)

TRAVELLING AROUND

From the airport there is a regular bus service to the centre of Faro, where it is possible to connect with train and bus services to the Algarve. However, both forms of transport tend to run more frequently in the early morning and late afternoon/early evening to accommodate the needs of the local people, and you should be prepared for a long wait.

Car

The easiest way to get around and access the walks in this book is by car. Car hire is cheap, especially in the winter months. Besides the large car hire companies offering car rentals there are many smaller ones that are just as good (and in many instances much cheaper). The best way to find these is to use your search engine and type in 'Algarve Car Rental'. Many of the airlines also offer car rental packages, so it is also worth enquiring when booking your flights.

Note that the accident rate on Portugal's main roads is high, and

dangerous overtaking is common. Impatient drivers try to force slower ones onto the hard shoulder, but it is strictly illegal to drive on the hard shoulder, even though you may see some drivers doing so. Use of seat belts is compulsory, and there are on-the-spot fines for non-use and for other offences including not carrying your driving licence and passport if a driver from another country. The car documents must also be in the car at all times.

Speed limits are:
- motorways – 120kmph
- main roads – 90kmph
- built-up areas – 60kmph
- towns – 40kmph

Buses

Local buses are too infrequent to make them a viable alternative to the car. The only exception to this is the coastal path between Lagos and Sagres, where there is a good bus service to and from Lagos and Monchique, which can be reached by bus from Portimao.

Banks
Usually open 08.30–14.45 Monday to Friday. Closed Saturday and Sunday.

Chemists
Farmacias are open during normal shopping hours; in larger resorts there is always one on duty 24 hours.

Emergencies
For all emergency services dial **112** and ask for: *policia, bombeiros* (fire service) or *ambulancia*.

Festivals
Official public holidays are as follows:
1 January, Shrove Tuesday (variable),
25 April, 1 May, 10 June, 15 August,
5 October, 1 November, 8 December and 25 December.

Hospitals and Medical Centres
Many of the larger resorts have private English-speaking medical centres. Many towns have a public health centre – *Centro da Saude* – where you can get treated, but do remember to take your passport. There are hospitals at Faro (tel: 289 891 100), Portimão (tel: 282 450 300) and Lagos (tel: 282 770 100).

Markets
The local town markets are open Monday to Saturday 08.00–13.00.
   There are weekly markets in Quarteira on Wednesdays and Loulé on Saturdays. There are large monthly markets in the following towns:
Portimão – 1st Monday
Alvor – 2nd Tuesday
Odiaxere – 4th Monday
Lagos – 1st Saturday
Silves – 3rd Monday
Almancil – 1st and 4th Sunday
Albufeira – 1st and 3rd Tuesday
Sagres – 1st Friday

Police
The telephone numbers of the main police stations are:
Faro – 289 887 605
Lagos – 282 762 809
Olhão – 289 701 457
Portimão – 282 422 440
Tavira – 281 322 022

Post Offices
Correios are identified by the letters CTT, and there is one in most towns and the larger villages. Opening hours are generally 09.00–12.00 and 14.00–18.00, but this can vary, and in the large towns the main office stays open all day, Monday to Friday *selos* or stamps can also be bought at tobacconists and some shops that sell postcards.

Shops
The supermarkets and shops in the main shopping centres are open all day, everyday. In the towns most of the shops close between 13.00–15.00 Monday to Friday and are only open on Saturday morning.

Telephones
The majority of phone boxes only accept phone cards, which can be bought at tobacconists and some post offices.

Toilets
Few public toilets exist, although the number is increasing. The signs are often pictoria, but note the difference between *Senhors* (Men) and *Senhoras* (Women), *Homens* is more commonly used for Men.

WHERE TO STAY

Hotels can be found almost all the way along the Algarve's coastal strip. In geographical terms the resort of Albufeira is roughly in the centre, but is very popular for package holidays and is likely to be busy. For this reason (and in terms of accessibility to the walks) it would be better to base yourself nearer to Carvoeiro. In addition to the Algarve's hotels, there are increasing numbers of inns and *residencials* offering rooms, and these often have the advantage of being in quieter locations.

The increasing diversity of development means that there are far more opportunities to rent a property, from large villas with pools to small town houses. There is a great choice, and during the winter months rentals are at their lowest – so shop around.

If you prefer to camp there are large international campsites at Albufeira, Aljezur, Praia da Luz, Lagos, Armaçao de Pera and Faro – they are open all winter. Camping and caravanning away from official sites is strictly forbidden, especially on beaches.

The internet is a good place to find accommodation. Probably the best overall information websites for the Algarve are: www.portugal-info.net and www.algarve-info.com and www.portugalresident.com.

GEOLOGY AND SCENERY

The relationship between scenery and underlying rock structure is clearly evident in the Algarve. There are three distinct areas, each with its own characteristic scenery and vegetation: the mountains of the north; the central limestone hills, known locally as the *barrocal;* and the coastal strip in the south.

The Mountains

The Serra – or mountainous zone – stretches across the north of the Algarve and occupies just over 7% of its total area, with 390km^2 of the land rising above 400m (*Walks 9, 10, 11*). A major part of this area is the distinctive zone known as the Serra de Monchique, which includes the peak of Foia (902m), the highest point in the region. Just 6km to the east on the same range is the peak of Picota (774m), the second-highest point. This mountain range was formed from intrusions of granite-type rocks during the Tertiary era, about 50 million years ago. The resulting rock – which is well exposed and can be clearly seen from the road as you drive up to Monchique – is very hard wearing and was once used in the form of small cubes for road building. Today it is still quarried at Nave close to Monchique, but most of it is exported.

Just south of the Monchique mountains, and extending eastwards to the Spanish border, is an extensive range of hills where the underlying rock is a mixture of Carboniferous shales and gritstone (*Walks 5, 6, 14, 21, 25–34*). In the east these hills are known as the Serra do Caldeirão, and form a rolling landscape with long high ridges and deeply dissected valleys. There are a number of peaks which exceed 400m, the highest being Pelados (589m). In the west on the Atlantic coast the shales and gritstones are well exposed in the cliffs.

The hills of the Serra do Caldeirão were once thickly forested with both cork and holm oak, but whole areas were stripped during the 15th century when oak was needed for shipbuilding during the Portuguese voyages of discovery. This led to massive soil erosion during extensive heavy

WALKING IN THE ALGARVE

winter rains and to the silting up of river estuaries. During World War I further deforestation occurred in an attempt to grow more wheat to augment dwindling food supplies. At first this was successful, but because of the shallow topsoil yields rapidly diminished. Today the local people try to eke out a living growing some cereals, vegetables and fruit, while raising sheep and goats.

The Barrocal Limestone
Walks 16, 17, 18, 19, 20, 22, 23
The central limestone hills form a lens-shaped area extending from Cape St Vincent in the west almost to the Spanish border in the east. The limestone is widest in the central Algarve, tapering off to both east and west. The rock is of variable age – from the Jurassic (133–135 million years ago) to the Miocene (5 million years ago) era – resulting in differences in composition throughout the region. The purest was used to make quicklime for whitewashing houses, which was done several times a year – today it is cheaper to use whitewash produced by local paint companies – and there are still large areas dotted with limekilns, particularly around São Bras de Alportel and Alte. The limestone tends to form a series of escarpments which run east–west, parallel to the mountain ranges. Rocha de Pena is the highest of these and the most striking, with vertical cliffs on both the north and south sides.

The word *barrocal* (from *barro*: 'clay', or 'land yielding clay' and *cal*: 'lime') usually refers to a barren, hilly landscape supporting only maquis-type vegetation, or a wasteland that cannot be cultivated. In the Algarve nothing could be further from the truth; here the *barrocal* is a highly productive area where almonds, olives, figs, carobs and many other crops are grown. The flora too is outstandingly diverse. Rocha de Pena is a prime example and is now a classified site (an area of particular scientific significance; the classification helps prevent development or destruction).

Coastal Zone
Walks 1, 2, 3, 7, 8, 15
The coastal (littoral) zone occupies just over 20% of the area of the Algarve, and most lies below 70m. It contains sedimentary rocks from the Tertiary era (2–60 million years ago) interspersed with younger sands. In the east around Faro these sands were deposited by the ocean and today form sand banks and dunes. In the west the sands are continuously deposited by the local rivers and have silted up various river mouths, including the Arade and Alvor.

As a consequence the coastal scenery is very different in the east and west. From Faro to the Spanish border there are long beaches of sand and gravel and chains of islands and sandspits. Behind these a lagoon of brackish water has formed, and inland there are extensive saltmarshes. Some

On the beach (Walk 3)

of these marshes have been drained and developed, but many are now protected in the Rio Formosa Nature Park. West of Faro the coast is characterised by multi-coloured cliffs which often feature on postcards; the cliff coastline, especially when it features caves, blow holes, rock arches and bridges, makes for stunning and spectacular scenery.

The coastal area was almost entirely agricultural until the late 1960s, when tourist development meant that large areas were lost to hotels, villa complexes and golf courses. Ten years later the government began to realise that much of the coastal region was under threat. In 1976 the saltmarshes around Castro Marim and Vila Real in the east became a protected area, but in the west the extensive area

of coastline from near Sagres to Sines in the Alentejo (70,000ha, of which 25,850ha are in the Algarve) came under the control of the of the Sudoeste Alentejano e Costa Vicentina Natural Park in 1988. Despite its protected status, developers continue to make inroads into this particularly beautiful area.

WILD FLOWERS

The Algarve's wide variety of soil types and habitats, and mild and sunny climate, combine to produce an astonishing range of flowering plants and shrubs. These are at their best from February to June, when the whole landscape – from the highest mountains to the coastal cliffs – is enriched by blazes of colour. Even during the height of summer, when much of the

19

landscape is brown and scorched, the sea daffodil and bright reddish-purple flowers of the stemless thistle can still be seen. In September and October the flowering season begins again, and the tall spikes of the sea squill shoot up from their enormous bulbs before the leaves emerge.

There are literally thousands of species to delight the eye. Many are endemics and not always easy to find in the standard guides, although several books are very useful, including: *Field Guide to the Wild Flowers of Southern Europe* by P. Davies and B. Gibbons (Crowood Press) and *Wild Flowers of Southern Europe* by B. Press and B. Gibbons (New Holland Publishers).

The flowers below are described according to their habitat.

The Mountains

As one might expect there are fewer species in this region, and distinct differences between the Monchique mountains and the hills of shale and gritstone. Up around Monchique the landscape is dominated by trees. There are cork oaks, olives, pines and new plantations of eucalyptus, with the occasional grove of sweet chestnut. In May tree heathers and camellias add a dash of colour, together with the bright purple flowers of the rhododendron bush (*ponticum sp Baeticum* – this species grows only on the Iberian Peninsula). Both types of lavender – purple *Lavandula stoechas* and

green *Lavandula viridas* – together with foxgloves and primroses in damp places, stone crops, crimson clover and early purple orchids all grow here and can be seen on any of the walks. The endemic *Euphorbia moniquensis*, which only grows high up on Picota, is much harder to find. This delicate member of the spurge family stays hidden beneath the ferns that can cover much of the hillsides. The plant, characterised by a single stem with small rounded leaves, has yellow flowers that appear at the end of the stem, creating an umbrella-like effect.

By far the most abundant plant cover on the shale and gritstone hills is the gum cistus, which has large white flowers – usually with a splash of deep magenta on the base of each petal. The leaves are dark green and extremely sticky. Tree heathers, with deep pink-and-white flowers, add to the colour of the landscape, as do the striking scented yellow flowers of the acacia trees such as *Acacia dealbata* and *Acacia pycnantha*. These are often planted along the roadsides, particularly on the road from Portimão up to Monchique, and in late January/early February are an especially fine sight. The strawberry tree, *Arbutus unedo,* grows everywhere and in early winter can be seen bearing both pale flowers and fruits, the latter darkening to a deep red when fully ripe. The fruits are used to make the local firewater, *medronho*.

Among the smaller plants that thrive in the shale and gritstone areas

Spring flowers at Ingrina (Walk 8)

are both types of lavender, wild gladiolus, wild nasturtiums and violets. An endemic plant in the shales, also seen in sandy places on the coast, is the Portuguese milky-white vetch, a perennial herb growing up to 1m high. It blooms from January to May and has very distinct creamy white flowers which grow from a central stem. It is poisonous to both sheep and cattle. In early spring large colonies of the tiny hooped-petticoat narcissus can be seen covering some of the shale cliffs in the Vila do Bispo area.

The Barrocal Limestone

The hilly areas of the *barrocal* are characterised by mastic and turpentine bushes, rosemary, lavender, dwarf fan palms, grey-leaved cistus, asphodels and wild asparagus, as can be seen at Rocha de Pena. Smaller flowers among the rocks and boulders include the paper white narcissus and a miniature daffodil.

Between the hills, where more cultivation has taken place, there are thousands of almond trees – now mostly abandoned, with the nuts left to rot on the branches. Other trees include olive, carob, fig, walnut and nespera or loquat. Along the roadsides pepper trees, cypresses, oleanders, Judas trees and pelargoniums abound.

The species that grow on the limestone are too numerous to list, but among the most ubiquitous is the Bermuda buttercup, which in spring makes beautiful golden carpets beneath

the almond trees (but is a noxious weed as far as horticulturists are concerned). Other favourites are field daisies, crown daisies, marguerites, vetch, field gladioli, aromatic inula, wild honeysuckles, common mallow and wild peony.

Coastal Zone

Because of the diversity of habitats, including the saltmarshes, there is an even greater variety of plants along the coast. One striking plant is the imported but naturalised *Agave Americana* or century plant. This has very sharp leaf edges so makes an effective barrier; after 10–15 years it grows a very tall, mast-like flower spike, and then dies. On the west coast along the cliff tops where sand dunes abound (formed from sands washed out from glaciers during the ice age) many rare plants grow, including *Antirrhinum major,* the ancestor of the cultivated snap dragon, and spectacular broomrape parasite species including the large yellow restharrow.

Orchids flourish on the lime-rich soils of the coastal areas. Many are insect-mimicry species, including the bee, brown bee, bumble bee and yellow bee orchids. These mimic the appearance and pheromones of female bees in order to attract males and increase their chances of pollination. Other orchids include the green-winged, naked man, pyramidal, woodcock and sawfly. Another striking spring flower is the tiny 'Barbary nut', *Gynandiris sisyrinchium.* The tiny blue flower resembles an iris and

Agave Americana in full bloom (Walk 12)

opens only from late morning to mid-afternoon; one is never ceased to be amazed at the wonder of nature when seeing these delicate plants poking through rock-hard soils. All the plants and flowers in the central limestone region are also found on the coastal strip, making this a very special place to walk during spring.

The area around Cape St Vincent (Sagres Peninsula) has many endemic plants, thriving in the wild windswept landscape. The gum cistus (usually with plain white flowers) dominates large areas, along with Buckler mustard (*Biscutella vincentina*), squill (*Scilla vincentina*) and toadflax (*Linaria algarviana*). The shrubby violet and 'Spanish' iris are found locally, as well as spectacular mounds of strongly scented thyme. Brilliant clumps of the shrubby pimpernel line the roadsides, while a very spiny bladder senna thrives in the fissured limestone around Sagres.

BIRDS, WILDLIFE AND PROTECTED AREAS

The fine climate, rich variety of habitats, and position at the southwestern corner of Europe all combine to make the Algarve a haven for many birds. Over 200 species inhabit the area or pass through it during spring and summer migrations. Bird enthusiasts visit during these times, keeping watch on the sea cliffs at Cape St Vincent to observe the passage of gannets, skuas, terns, shearwaters and other seabirds. For the interested walker, many seabirds are resident and can readily be seen in the areas described below.

Away from the coast – and especially in the northern hills – one bird likely to catch the eye is the azure-winged magpie, with its bright blue wings and long blue tail. On many of the hill walks, particularly near woodland, woodpeckers are frequently heard calling but are not often seen. There are three species: green, greater-spotted and lesser spotted. These areas are also good for crested tits.

The scrubland of the *barrocal* and lower hill slopes makes an ideal habitat for small songbirds, which seem to delight in hiding themselves before they can be identified. Sardinian warblers are everywhere, stonechats are often seen perched on top of a long stalk, and flocks of goldfinches a frequent sight. Black redstarts are common, as are chiffchaffs, meadow pipits, robins and blackbirds. Crag martins are abundant near the coast, with shags, cormorants and many species of gull.

Of particular interest are the many storks that nest on town chimneys as well as treetops and electricity pylons. Other exotic birds to be seen are large colonies of flamingos and the avocets. More rare is the purple gallinule – a large bird with purple-blue plumage – but it can be spotted at one or two of the nature reserves in the area (see below).

Although the bird population is predominant in the Algarve, there are a number of wild animals that should be mentioned. Still in existence (but very rare) are the wolf and the badger. The fox is becoming rare too, but has been seen on several occasions while researching this book. More common is the ring-tailed civet cat that preys on poultry. Rabbits are more abundant than hares, but both are hunted for sport and food. There is quite a large population of Egyptian mongoose, but they are generally nocturnal and not often seen; they are easily recognised by the long tail with a distinct tuft on the end resembling a pompom.

Reptiles are present in quantity, but in fewer numbers than in the eastern Mediterranean. The Moorish gecko is common and found near houses and ruins. The most likely lizards to be seen are the spiny-footed, Iberian wall and the large green ocellated species. Snakes usually vanish quickly into the undergrowth; the only venomous one is the very uncommon Lataste's viper. More readily spotted are the grass snake, viperine, ladder and horseshoe whip snakes, southern smooth and false smooth snakes, plus the huge Montpelier which often grows to 2m.

In the scrubland butterflies are numerous, with many skippers, blues and fritillaries. The swallowtail and scarce swallowtail are commonly seen, and where the *Arbutus* bush grows the two-tailed pasha is found during May and late summer.

Nature Reserves and Protected Sites
Walks 3, 7, 8

Throughout Portugal there are numerous protected areas, including national parks, natural parks, nature reserves, protected countryside and classified sites. In the Algarve the largest protected area stretches all the way along the west coast from Sines to Sagres, and then eastwards to Burgau. This 70,000ha area was designated to protect the unique flora, and also extends to a 2km maritime area known as Area de Paisagem Protegida do Sudoeste Alentejano e Costa Vicentina. Close to Faro the 18,400ha Parque Natural da Ria Formosa protects the delicate flora and fauna of the saltmarshes which stretch for 60km from Ancão near Quinta do Lago to Cacela a Velha. Within the park there is the integral Quinta de Marim with its large information, research and bird rehabilitation centres. The Reserve Natural do Sapal de Castro Marim e Vila Real de Santo Antonio in the eastern Algarve has an information centre in the castle at Castro Marim. This reserve again preserves marshes and working saltpans, home to many wetland birds including the greater flamingo, spoonbills and avocets. Classified sites which do offer limited protection include the Fonte de Benemola and Rocha da Pena.

Cork

Walks 10, 11, 23, 25–33

The evergreen oak, *Quercus suber*, is very important in the Portuguese economy. Portugal supplies over half the world's cork. and is the most wooded of all Mediterranean countries (39% cover), having about 3 million hectares of forest, and cork trees make up about a quarter of the forest area. Often the plantings are irregular, but such is the value of the product that even single trees are grown commercially. In the Algarve the most important centres of cork-oak production are (in descending order of importance)in the *concelhos* of Loulé, Monchique, Silves, São Bras de Alportel and Aljezur, and the total afforested area of cork oak in the region is close to 42,000ha.

The economic cork is derived from the outer bark of the tree, which is stripped during the summer months. Skilled workers use a razor-sharp machete to make horizontal incisions right around the tree, and then link these with vertical cuts. The bark is carefully removed without damaging the trunk beneath, and the last two digits of the year are painted on in white paint; '04' indicates the tree was last stripped in 2004. Skilled workers can cut from 150–400kg of cork a day. The first cutting of 'virgin cork' occurs once the tree reaches about 25 years; it is usually low quality, but further removals of cork are made at about nine-year intervals until the tree is finally exhausted at about 170 years.

Cork collection (Walk 11)

After the sections of bark have been stripped they are piled up for initial curing, and then taken to cork collection points. From here they are transported to factories and boiled in water for several hours to make them flexible, then flattened and stored until required.

Eucalyptus
Walks 5, 6, 9, 11, 13, 14
The planting of this fast-maturing species to provide pulp for the paper industry is a controversial matter. The economic advantages are obvious, and Portugal needs the income, but local farmers and environmentalists are concerned about the effects on the water table, the increased fire risk and the depletion of soil nutrients.

The species most often planted is *E. globules* spp *Globules*, which has single flowers. There are large plantations in the syenite area of Monchique, where the seedlings are densely planted and coppiced after eight years. Regrowth is fast, and after thinning the new shoots are left for another eight years and coppiced again. After about 30 years the trees are replanted. In the Algarve eucalyptus timber is also used in the building industry for scaffolding poles, and for beams and roof trusses.

Pine
Walks 3, 4, 5, 15
Pine is grown for both turpentine and timber in coastal areas as well as in the hills. Both *Pinus pinaster* and *Pinus*

pinea are used in shipbuilding and for constructing mule carts (*carroças*). The large fleets of caravels, *naus* and galleons used in the explorations of Henry the Navigator in the 15th century had resinous pinewood in the keels and stem and other parts where water penetrates, while the ribs of the ships were usually made of cork oak and holm oak.

The mule carts were an important part of the traditional integrated agricultural system of the Algarve, but there is little place for them in an era of increasing motor traffic, although many older farmers as well as gypsies still favour them. *Pinus pinea*, the stone pine or umbrella pine, is also grown for pine nuts, especially near the coast.

Chestnuts
Walk 11
Chestnuts are not native to the Algarve, but have been grown over the slopes of the Monchique hills since the 1820s. However, during the early 20th century many trees were lost to blight. The chestnuts rival the better-known Spanish nuts in both size and quality, but the trees are cultivated much more for their wood. This is prized for making beds and other furniture because of its superb grain and colour, as well as its strength.

Charcoal
Walks 9, 10, 11, 25–33
Typical of the Serra, including around Monchique, is the production of charcoal. This is made by the slow

Young eucalyptus (Walk 5)

burning of a mound of wood for about 10 days, the correct rate of burning being maintained by drilling air holes through the pile as necessary. Large sheets of bark on the surface of the heap prevent too much air getting in. The charcoal is used mainly as fuel for open grills and barbecues.

Traditional Fruit Trees
Walks 4, 12, 16, 17, 18, 19, 22, 23, 24
Small-scale farming is the normal practice in the Algarve, unlike the Alentejo to the north where vast plains of cereals and cork oaks are grown. These small farms, mainly in the *barrocal* limestone area and in the eastern littoral, grow various combinations of Mediterranean fruit trees with an under-planting of cereals or grass for grazing animals, and small fields of peas and beans. The trees chosen are those that, once established, require little or no watering and are easy to look after: fig, olive, carob and almond, as well as vines.

Figs were once very important to the rural economy and many tons were exported. Now many of the trees are neglected, but they are still a feature of the winter landscape with pale grey bare branches upturned at the ends. One reason for this decline is the selling of land to developers. Another is that as the older generation of farmers die they are not replaced, as their offspring prefer to look to the towns and tourist developments for work. Olives, and olive oil production, are also declining for similar

reasons. The silvery grey foliage is always a delight to the eye, as are the gnarled and twisted forms of the old trees, which can live to 1000 years and more. Carobs, like olives, are evergreen. Their fruits are long pods which turn black/brown when ripened in the sun. The fruits have a high protein content and are an invaluable source of animal fodder, as well as being used to produce an edible gum used in foodstuffs.

The flowering of the almond trees in January and February is one of the great sights of the Algarve. About the end of August (after the fig harvest but before that of olives), almonds are knocked off the trees with long canes. By this time the sun has split open the outer husk, exposing the shell containing the nut, and many more husks break off when the fruits hit the ground. Drying is traditionally carried out on the flat roofs of Algarve houses. Again, almond nut production has severely suffered with the encroachment of the tourist industry.

Small vineyards can be seen on many of the walks, both in the *barrocal* and in the coastal areas. Grapes grown in the Algarve are either for table use (*uvas de mesa*) or winemaking (*uvas de vinho*), or produced on a very small scale for drying (*passas de uva*). Most of the eating grapes are consumed by the growers or sold very quickly through the local markets. Some 80% of all wine produced in the Algarve is processed at one of four Adegas Cooperativas – in Lagôa, Tavira,

Threshing by hand (Walk 16)

Portimão and Lagos – and consumed locally.

Other Crops
Walks 16, 17, 22, 25–33

Maize and winter cereals, such as wheat and oats, are grown on many small farms. Winnowing is carried out on the spot, and threshing floors can be seen on several walks. They vary enormously in size and may be made of beaten earth, bricks, tiles or concrete. Rice is still produced near Aljezur and was formerly grown near Silves. Peas and broad beans are commonly planted in small fields near farmhouses, or below almonds and carobs. The broad bean, or *fava*, is a favourite of the local people and is served either as an accompaniment or as the basis of a main dish. More and more market gardens are starting up, growing a wide

variety of fruits and vegetables to help meet demand from residents and tourists alike.

Citrus Fruits
Walks 12, 16, 17

Unlike the traditional fruit trees, citrus fruit requires irrigation during the dry summer months and is always grown in areas with the highest rainfall. The construction of new reservoirs has enabled many new plantations to be developed on the coastal plains, although not too near the sea as the trees are not salt tolerant. The trees flower from March to May, filling the air with a heady perfume, and their fruits ripen from October onwards; in January and February, depending on the variety, they are picked. Most important are the sweet oranges, but tangerines, mandarins, clementines

30

and satsumas are also grown, as well as a few grapefruit. Lemon trees are grown as windbreaks for the more delicate orange trees, but their fruits are rarely picked.

Beekeeping
Walks 25–33
Honey is produced almost everywhere in the Algarve, and rows of beehives are a common sight. In the higher areas the bees forage among the eucalyptus, heathers, strawberry trees and acacias as well as the gum cistus; in the *barrocal* they collect the pollen of its numerous plants and herbs. Locally produced honey may be found for sale in markets and some shops, the best honey being that produced from the nectar of the green and French lavenders.

Irrigation
Walks 5, 12, 16, 17, 21, 22, 23, 24
In the interior of the Algarve where the land is cultivated numerous wells can be seen – almost every house and smallholding has its own. The deep circular wells, known as *noras*, were formerly operated by a blindfolded mule harnessed to a metal arm which pulled up a long chain of buckets. Most wells are now abandoned, having been replaced by electric pumps, and the water is used strictly for crops. The construction of large dams like the Barragem da Bravura and Barragem do Silves has created reservoirs which help to provide water during summer months. Water is distributed via a series of irrigation channels that lead from the reservoirs and can extend for many kilometres over the countryside.

Beehive made out of cork (Walks 31 and 33)

HISTORY

Throughout the Algarve there is widespread evidence that the area was inhabited by early peoples. On several of the walks solitary standing stones – menhirs – can be seen; there are a large number close to Vila do Bispo in the area known as Montes dos Amantes. These, together with stone tools, have been dated to the Neolithic period (5000–2700BC). At Alcalar to the north of Portimão there is a megalithic grave (or tumulus) dated around 2000–600BC. It consists of a circular stone chamber and corridor which have now been fully excavated and are open to visitors.

The Romans arrived in the Algarve about 218BC and stayed for the next 600 years. Their most lasting mark on the Algarvian landscape was the road system; the routes of many Roman roads are still used today.

The Romans built towns and bridges, improved castles and defences, and started small industries such as fish-salting stations. Some of these fish tanks have been restored at Quinta Marim, the visitor centre for the Rio Formosa Nature Park.

The greatest influence on the landscape came from the North African Moors who invaded the Iberian Peninsula in AD711. They were responsible for the introduction of wells, water wheels and the agricultural system. The Moors gave the Algarve its name, 'Al Gharb', meaning 'western land', and were responsible for a style of architecture that is still in use today – low white buildings and rounded arches, blue and white tiles or *azulejos,* and the highly decorative filigree chimney pots. The Moorish capital was Silves, then known as Chelb. It was

The Roman bridge over the Quarteira river (Walk 18)

an important and civilised town and trading area, with direct access to the sea by the Arade river. In its heyday the population was well over 3000, and it was said to be like Baghdad, with mosques, bazaars and many citrus orchards. Now the river is silted up and not navigable. When Silves fell in 1189 to a combined attack from the King of Portugal, Dom Sancho I, and crusaders from England and Germany, it was the beginning of the end of Moorish domination.

In 1249 King Alfonso II of Portugal finally brought an end to the rule of the Moors, and subsequent rulers were always known as 'Kings [or Queens] of Portugal and the Algarve', an acknowledgement of the separate identity of the Algarve. (This practice continued until the overthrow of the monarchy in 1910.) In subsequent years there were many disputes with and challenges to the Portuguese kingdom from Castile, which must be omitted from this short account. However, one particularly significant event was the marriage of King João I to Philippa, the daughter of John O'Gaunt, from which began the long alliance of Portugal with England. In the 15th century it was their son Henry 'The Navigator' who instigated and sponsored the great voyages of exploration which were made from the Algarvian ports of Sagres and Lagos. Madeira and the Azores were discovered; gradually the western coast of Africa was followed further and further south, culminating after Henry's

death with the rounding of the Cape of Good Hope by Bartolomeu Dias in 1488 and Vasco da Gama's voyage to Calcutta in 1498.

In 1755 a massive earthquake badly affected the area, and many buildings were destroyed, not only in the Algarve but also in the Alentejo and Lisbon. A tidal wave 20m high drowned many local people and deposited large amounts of sand in harbours and river mouths. Minor earthquakes are still common in the area today.

In 1807 Portugal was invaded by Napoleon, and during the Peninsular War British and Portuguese troops under the command of Wellington drove the French out of Portugal. In 1910 the monarchy was ended and a republic proclaimed, heralding a period of turmoil with great economic difficulties. By 1928 control had fallen into the hands of Salazaar, first as Minister of Finance and then as Prime Minister, who established a dictatorship parallel to that of Franco in Spain. This time of great poverty and little personal freedom continued until the 'Carnation' revolution of 1974. In the late 1960s Salazaar became ill (he died in 1970) and was replaced by Caetano, who was not a strong personality. Unrest among the people grew and came to the fore on 25 April when a coup by MFA (the Armed Forces Movement) overthrew Caetano. This was an almost completely bloodless revolution in which soldiers carried carnations in the barrels of their rifles.

Things were not plain sailing after this. During the first, moderate, phase there were three provisional governments. In 1975 a more radical phase began, and the fourth provisional government decreed large-scale nationalisation of private monopolies. Eventually the radical elements became so divided amongst themselves that increasingly conservative elements took over. In 1976 elections took place and constitutional government began. The principles of a pluralist democracy were established, and the people found themselves with greater political freedom than they had ever known. The painful return to democracy was rewarded by admission to the European Community in 1986, and in 2002 Portugal became one of 12 member states to adopt the Euro as its currency (in place of the Escudo).

NOTES FOR WALKERS

Nature of the Walks

Most walks in the book make use of old mule or cart tracks, which until recently were the only means of communication between villages. Underfoot the going varies; some tracks have been covered in bitumen or asphalt, others are smooth earth, while many are rough and stony. Most of the walks are not particularly strenuous, ascents of 500m being about the maximum, and none could be considered difficult. They vary in length between 2.5km and 17km.

Maps

The Algarve is covered by 14 sheets in the Carta Geografico do Portugal 1:50,000 series published in the late 1960s and early 1970s. These maps unfortunately do not include the enormous changes that have occurred since then. Besides the large-scale developments along the coast many new roads have been created, especially since Portugal joined the EC. Some roads are completely new and cut across the countryside; others follow old paths and tracks that have been upgraded to drivable roads – none of these changes are on the maps. Similarly some paths and tracks that feature on these maps have disappeared altogether from a combination of disuse and encroaching vegetation.

The Algarve is also covered by 39 sheets of the 1:25,000 maps of Portugal produced by the Instituto Geografico do Exercito (www.igeoe.pt), Av. Dr Alfredo Bensaude, 1849–014 Lisbon, tel: +351 218 505 300, fax: +351 218 532 119. They cannot be bought in the Algarve, but are available in the UK: Stanfords (www.stanfords.co.uk). However, the series is not updated or revised on a regular basis, and some maps are very out of date.

Waymarking

The only walks in the area that are officially waymarked are those in the Serra do Caldeirão. You will see coloured marks along some of the walks, together with coloured arrows, but these are often used to show the way to houses that are off the beaten track. Land boundaries are marked by small stone or cement blocks that can be confused for waymarks. Follow the directions in the book at all times to avoid possible confusion.

Access

After the peaceful revolution of 1974 the large country estates of Portugal – mainly in the Alentejo but also in the northern Algarve – were divided and distributed among the people. Boundaries were marked by stone posts bearing the initials of the owner or, in some cases, by cairns with white-painted stones. Walkers must be aware that these cairns represent land boundaries and should not expect them to indicate a footpath, as they do in many other countries.

Fenced land is not common except where there are orchards and market gardens (especially near towns), and fences occasionally enclose land where animals such as goats are being reared. In some areas of the *barrocal* there are stone walls of considerable thickness, built with stones from land clearance for arboriculture rather than from a desire to keep people out.

The local people are very friendly, but cannot understand why people would like to go walking. On several occasions during my research people have came to stand in their doorways to watch me pass by. There is no law of trespass and 'Private' notices are rare, but if you do come across them please respect the owner's wishes – the notices invariably belong not to the Portuguese but to foreigners.

Information board, Feiteira (Walks 28-30)

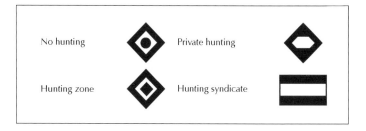

| No hunting | | Private hunting | |
| Hunting zone | | Hunting syndicate | |

Hunting

Hunting is still a popular national pastime. In 1988 laws were passed regularising what had been a chaotic situation, with unlicensed shooting over vast areas by large numbers of people. Since then those who want to hunt must apply for a licence and pass a test. The hunting season runs from September to the end of February. Hunting zones are defined, and hunting restricted to Thursdays, Sundays and national holidays. During the season it is not advisable to walk on these days as accidents can – and do – happen. Wild boar, rabbits, hares, foxes and all kinds of birds, including songbirds, are the target for the hunters.

Various signs in red and white have been erected on some boundaries and relate to hunting, not to walking. The most common ones that you will see are illustrated above.

Bees

Beehives are everywhere, and it is safer to give them a wide berth. I have been stung several times, and on one occasion was attacked by a large swarm. The best treatment is to remove the sting immediately with tweezers. If you are allergic to bee stings do take medication with you.

Dogs

While walking in the Algarve you will see and hear many dogs, though only rarely are they ferocious. I have been bitten once, and that was by a small dog who launched her teeth into the back of my calf! If you are frightened of dogs or if one appears menacing you must do what the Portuguese do; pick up a stone and threaten to throw it. Imaginary stones often do the trick in the absence of the real thing.

River Crossings

Throughout the year most streams are almost or completely dry. However, after heavy rain the same streams can be swollen to an unimaginable degree, sometimes as much as 3m above the normal low level. It is self-evident that walks which involve any river crossings cannot be attempted in these circumstances.

Car Thefts

Never ever leave anything of any value in a car, not even while away for 'five minutes'.

Equipment and Clothing

In the winter dress as for reasonable summer conditions in Britain. A light sweater is often necessary in the morning and at the end of the day. Windproof fleeces or waterproof jackets are insurance against the odd shower or in windy conditions. Lightweight boots are suitable for all the walks, and for many walking shoes are adequate. Snow is almost unheard of, and many young people in the Algarve have never seen it. When it rains, it usually does so for 4–5 hours, so it is best to forget walking and do something else.

Do not underestimate the power of the sun, even during the winter months. Make sure you have adequate sun protection, including a hat, and always carry plenty of water.

Emergencies

Many walkers today carry a phone in case of emergencies. However, mobile phones may not work in more remote areas or in particular parts of the Serra de Caldeirão, so do not rely on it. If you can get a signal the number to call is **112**; this is equivalent to 999 in Britain. Ask for someone who speaks English, and they will assess your situation and organise help. There is currently no charge for this service, but make sure that you are suitably insured.

Fires

Please remember the Algarve becomes extremely dry during the summer months and there is always a serious risk of fire. It is forbidden to light a fire outdoors between June and October.

Warning

While the author has made every effort to ensure the accuracy of the routes in this guide, a book of this nature is more prone to become inaccurate than a general guidebook. Changes to roads and tracks can occur at any time, the most common being changes to the surfacing of tracks and paths. So if you are following a route on a track, and all seems to be going well, then it suddenly becomes a surfaced road that is not mentioned in the guide, you are probably still on the right route (especially if the surface looks new).

Using the Guide

The routes in this guide are arranged from west to east, starting on the western Atlantic coast and heading east across the region towards the Spanish border.

At the beginning of each route is a box giving the walk's distance, timing and grade, together with details of refreshment facilities and how to access the start of the walk. The timings are intended as a guide only, and do not take into account stops en route.

The distances and heights given in the walk were obtained from a GPS.

Some of the walks could be linked together, and where this is possible it is indicated in the text.

Walk Grades

The walks have been graded in terms of the amount of climbing involved:

Easy – no ascents – a level walk suitable for all abilities.
Moderately easy – some climbing involved, but nothing too taxing.
Moderately difficult – some fairly strenuous ascents and/or steep descents.
Difficult – a challenging walk with a number of strenuous ascents and descents.

The beautiful Zambujal river (Walk 34)

WALK 1

Esteveira

Distance	2.5km/1.6 miles
Time	1hr
Grade	Easy
Facilities	Cafés in Rogil, and several restaurants closer to Aljezur on the N120.
Access	Drive north from Aljezur on the N120 to Rogil. At the far end of the village turn left at the sign for Esteveira; follow the road until the surface ends (about 3km). There is a small parking area on the right.

Esteveira is a small nature reserve on the west coast north of Aljezur. It is an area of dunes perched high on top of the cliffs and the habitat is extremely fragile. There are few signs to this completely unspoilt area (another good way of preserving the habitat!) so it is virtually ignored by tourists. Plants found here include antirrhinums, Hottentot figs, Portuguese milky white vetch, several rock roses, sparkling blue lithospermum and sage-leaved cistus. It is important to keep to the footpaths to avoid trampling the vegetation. The walk also offers outstanding views of the sea and cliffs. A real treat.

Walk along the track to the left that passes between **two cottages**, and soon you will notice a steep ravine on your right. When the now sandy track heads downhill take a sandy path off to the left which leads to the clifftop.

A short walk around a nature reserve with stunning coastal scenery.

Numerous paths cross the reserve and you are free to explore. However, the walk itself follows the path that runs parallel to the cliff edge, leading to a flat shelf with wonderful views along the coast northwards; on a clear day you can see as far as Sines.

Follow the path around to the left and soon you come to another shelf with more superb views, this time southwards. Continue along the clifftop until you reach a small wet area where tall giant reeds stand out above the

39

Spring flowers in Esteveira nature reserve

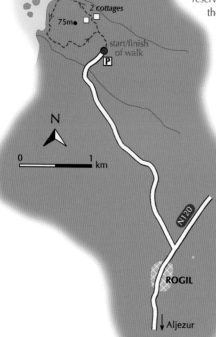

general vegetation; the path turns inland to go around them.

When you meet a second ravine ahead (the southern margin of the reserve) the path leads away from the sea towards an area of pine trees. The path now wanders through the pinewood and then is obstructed by a simple fence erected by a local farmer. Follow the fence up to the left and find a path to the right which passes downhill (between the farmers' fences) and through a field to the road. Turn left and walk down the road back to your car.

WALK 2
Pontal, Carrapateira and Vilharinha

Distance	16km/10 miles; short walk 6km/3.7 miles
Time	5hrs; short walk 2hrs
Grade	Moderately easy; short walk – easy
Facilities	Good selection of cafés and restaurants in/close to Carrapateira. Several houses now offer 'rooms'; small guest house.
Access	Carrapateira is 13km from Vila do Bispo along the N268 going towards Aljezur. As you approach the village there is a signed road to the left to 'Praia do Amado'; turn left and follow the road down to the parking area above the beach.

Pontal is a headland on the West Atlantic coast with multi-coloured cliffs and spectacular coastal scenery: numerous bays and headlands, offshore stacks and rocky islands. To the north the headland is bordered by the large sandy beach and dunes of Praia da Bordeira, and to the south by the very beautiful Praia do Amado (Lovers' beach), popular with surf enthusiasts. Away from the coast you will find beautiful secluded valleys and steep hillsides, home to a rich variety of animal and birds.

The Pontal is very popular with Portuguese families at weekends, so it is best to avoid these if possible.

LONG WALK

With the sea behind you, walk back along the road until you reach a large information board on the right; take the track off to the right directly in front of it. This heads down to meet another track. Turn right; follow this track around the hillside and away from the sea before bearing left to pass through a small wood of eucalyptus and then stone pine trees. After about 25min the track rises to meet another good track. *The short walk goes left at this point.*

Spectacular coastal and country scenery. Jurassic limestone cliffs carved and shaped by the sea; at the far end of Amado beach stands Pedra do Cavaleiro; inland underlying schist rocks provide rolling countryside.

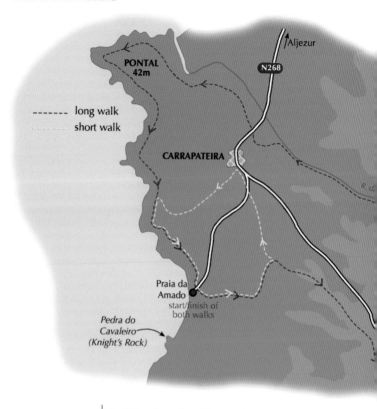

To follow the main walk turn right.

The track climbs gently up through the countryside before reaching a main road. Turn left and almost immediately take a road off to the right to **Vilharinha**. This quiet road offers tremendous views down to the valley on your right; you should soon be able to spot the small hamlet of Vilharinha, once abandoned but now being brought back to life.

The road begins to drop down to the valley and you pass several houses before the road begins to level out. Here you should see a wide track to the left (there may be a sign to the horse-riding stables 'Quinta Herdade'). Follow this track beside the small **Carrapateira river** for about 4km until you come to the main road. Cross over and take the surfaced road directly opposite, signed 'Praia'. Pass a café and a restaurant before the road rises on to the Pontal and the surface gives way to a wide dusty road. This leads around the headland, but off to the left are paths that will take you close to the cliff edge before arriving at the trig point of **Pontal** (42m), close to a headland which is a favourite spot with local fisherman.

After the headland the road turns south. This stretch of coastline offers a rich variety of coastal scenery; there are plenty of opportunities to leave the road and follow footpaths close to the clifftops, but remember that parts are unstable, so do not stray too close to the edge.

About 4km from the headland the road regains its surface just before it descends to **Amado beach**.

SHORT WALK

Follow the long walk until the junction with the track and turn left (*the main walk goes right*). Follow the track down through the countryside; when you meet a track coming in from the left continue straight on. Soon you will arrive at a surfaced road leading to Amado beach; turn right and walk up towards the main road. Just before reaching the main road turn left on a small track. This runs parallel to the road before rising up to meet it. Turn left and walk along the road for about 20m before turning left onto a good track that passes below

Unusual cliff formation on the Pontal headland

the school house; across the road lies the small village square of **Carrapateira**.

Continue on this track for about 1.5km before bending sharp right to head uphill towards some buildings and a wide unsurfaced road (the road that passes around the Pontal headland). Across the junction is a café and restaurant. Turn left and follow the road back to the car park, enjoying superb views over Amado beach and the surrounding coastline.

WALK 3

The West Coast

LONG WALK

Distance	19km/11.8 miles
Time	6hrs
Grade	Moderate
Facilities	Cafés and restaurants in Vila do Bispo.
Access	Drive along the N125 towards Sagres and take the second exit for Vila do Bispo. At the roundabout follow the signs for the 'Mercado', and as you approach the second roundabout look for a parking space by the roadside.

Because the west coast between Vila do Bispo and Carrapateira is not readily accessible by car, the wild beauty of this coastline is often undiscovered by visitors. Compared with most of the Algarve the cliffs here are very different – they are almost black in colour and have a very sombre appearance. The short walk option below embraces part of the longer walk and can easily be done with children.

At the second roundabout take the first exit to the right, The road passes the 'Centro da Saude' on your left before bending sharp left. Follow the road until you almost reach the main 'Aljezur' road. Here there is a track on the left that heads uphill – take this. At the top of the rise take the path to the right, and keep on this until it meets the main road by a farmhouse. Turn left. Walk along the road for about 100m when you will see a track off to the left; turn left. The track bends almost immediately right to run parallel to the main road before meeting a track. Cross directly over onto a very grassy track that parallels the road until it meets another track and a sign for the 'Perimetro Florestal'; turn left.

Wonderfully varied coastal and countryside landscapes, but very different from Walk 2.

The view to the sea from Walk 3

Continue straight ahead, passing a wide track off to the left. Your track again runs parallel to the road as it passes a house with a tall wire fence on the left. As you approach an entrance to a villa the track bends sharp left; almost immediately you will see a sandy track off to the right. Turn right.

Follow the track past the villa and through a flat landscape

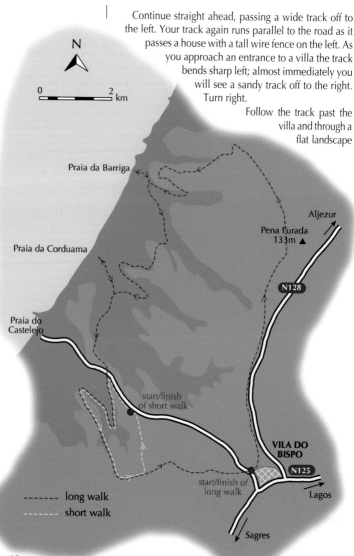

with a moorland feel; ahead you will see a windfarm and the trig point of **Pena Furada** (133m). When the track forks go left, soon reaching a wide track where you turn left. Head for a small copse of pine trees; ignore the track leading right as you approach the copse. Pass through the copse and meet another track coming in from the right. Continue straight on for about 1km to reach a crossroads of tracks. Turn left.

Just as the track begins to head downhill you will see a track off to the right; turn right to pass in front of a very isolated villa. Continue straight on (ignore any turnings to the right). The track becomes much stonier as it soon goes right to head towards the sea and a wonderful viewing point above **Barriga beach**.

The track rounds the hillside before descending to meet a wide track. Turn right and continue downhill to cross over a river bed (the track here has been concreted). *A track off to the right leads down to the beach.* To continue the walk go left and follow the track uphill.

The wide track rises and leads around the hillsides, with glimpses of the sea, before descending to meet a surfaced road; turn left (*if you turn right the road leads to* **Praia da Corduama**). Follow the road uphill and around to the left to meet a surfaced road (*which leads to* **Praia do Castelejo**). Cross the road and turn left, continue for about 20m and take a track off to the right. This winds down the hillside; when you see another good track off to the right turn right along it.

The track climbs up along the hillside; across the valley ahead you can see the sea. At the top of the rise meet another wide track; turn left so that your back is towards the sea. The track undulates before rising to meet a wide track/unsurfaced road; now turn left. Pass a large farmstead on the right after which you will see a track off to the right; ignore it and keep straight on.

When you come to a distinct fork in the road go right. Follow the road down and around until you meet another track; go left and soon you will be in **Vila do Bispo**. Walk down the road to find the roundabout at the start of the walk.

SHORT WALK

Distance	4km/2.5 miles
Time	1.5hrs
Grade	Easy
Facilities	Cafés and restaurants in Vila do Bispo.
Access	Follow the N125 towards Sagres and take the second exit for Vila do Bispo. Follow the signs for 'Praia do Castelejo' and after about 1.5km you will see signs to a picnic area on the left. Turn left to find the parking area.

This short walk gives you a flavour of the area and has great sea views.

Walk back towards the road and take the track off to the left, parallel to the road. Follow this until it drops down to the road where you will see another track off to the left; turn left. This track winds down the hillside; turn right when you see another good track off to the right.

This climbs up along the hillside; across the valley ahead you can see the sea. At the top of the rise meet another wide track; turn left so that your back is towards the sea. The track undulates before rising to meet a wide track/unsurfaced road; now turn left. Pass a large farmstead on the right after which you will see a track off to the right; ignore it and keep straight on.

When you come to a distinct fork in the road go left and follow the track/road back to the picnic area, ignoring several tracks off to the left.

Corduama beach

48

WALK 4
Bensafrim

Distance	10.4km/6.5 miles
Time	3hrs
Grade	Moderately easy. A river has to be forded twice, but it is never very deep.
Facilities	Several cafés in Bensafrim.
Access	If coming on the A22 drive westwards until the motorway finishes, then follow the signs into Bensafrim. At the first set of lights turn left, signed to the 'Mercado'; follow the road up and around to the right and you should find some parking spaces.

Although only 10km from Lagos very few tourists visit Bensafrim. The local inhabitants carry on with their lives at their own steady pace. This is a traditional Portuguese village; there is nothing remarkable about it. The church does have some valuable works of art, and there are Iron Age remains at Fonte Velha; both village and surrounding countryside give you a taste of the 'real' Algarve.

Walk along the road; at the crossroads turn left and follow the road down and over the bridge, continuing to the left for about 50m before turning left on to a track almost opposite the '**Casa de Santa Misericordia**'. Follow this track away from the village, passing several houses before bending around to the right (ignore a road to the left, which leads over a bridge).

Continue along this track for a good 3km. Tracks leads off both left and right but do not deviate unless you want to look at old ruins, passed en route. After passing one on the right with a great example of an old well the track begins to descend, with wonderful views over the countryside to the north.

At the bottom of the descent meet another track and turn right (not sharp right). The track follows the

A circular walk that fords a river several times and offers a wonderful insight into the true Algarve.

Bensafrim river on the left, with a large field of vines right, eventually descending to cross the water (usually via stepping stones). Continue along the track for another 100m or so until you meet another track; turn right.

Stay on this main track as it passes through unspoilt countryside where some farmers are attempting to establish vineyards. The track crosses another river

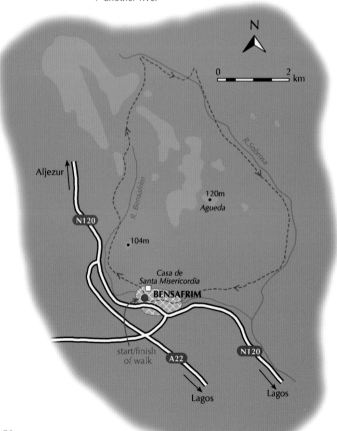

Looking towards Bensafrim

– the **Sobrosa**; continue to follow it, with the river now on the left, for quite a while before veering off right around the hillside. Once again, do not be tempted onto any other tracks that climb up to the right.

Your track comes close to the river once more before becoming a small surfaced road. After passing a horse riding centre on the right the road forks; turn right. Now follow the road all the way to the edge of the village, passing traditional and modern houses and farms along the way. Just before the edge of the village pass a large wash house on the left, and then the road forks. Go right to head up to the church, which you pass on the right. Now continue straight ahead. Very soon you will find yourself between two streets; take the right one. Proceed through the village before the old road drops slightly to a junction; cross straight over and the road will lead you back to your car.

WALK 5
The Barragem da Bravura

Distance	10km/6.2 miles
Time	3hrs
Grade	Moderately easy
Facilities	Hansel and Gretel restaurant and café at the start.
Access	Drive into the town of Odiaxere on the N125 (the first Odiaxere exit on the A22), and turn right at the lights in the centre. Follow the road through Odiaxere and around to the left (the *barragem* will be signed), and after 7km the lake will come into view. Drive down to the large parking area on the left by the Hansel and Gretel restaurant and café.

The *barragem* (dam) was built across the Bravura river in the late 1950s/early 1960s, to form a reservoir and so provide a consistent water supply to the coastal towns and villages. Behind the dam there is now an extensive lake, surrounded by rolling hills, a truly picturesque setting and a wonderful area for walking; all types of watersports and fishing are banned. However, the area is popular with local families at weekends for picnics, although in recent years a barrier has prevented the use of 4x4 vehicles around the lake margins so people tend to stay much closer to the road than before. The felling of eucalyptus trees and the associated use of heavy vehicles has tended to churn up some of the path.

A circular walk around part of the lake and through the surrounding countryside. Much of the area was under eucalyptus trees, but now there are moves to replant with 'stone' pines.

Looking at the lake from the car park, take the small road on the left that heads downhill towards a house. Just before the house cross the small drainage channel on the right onto a grassy area to pick up a path that passes in front of a small copse of pine trees. The path leads to some steps that descend to a road; turn left to walk down to the **dam**. Cross the dam and follow the track to the left on the far side.

Stay on this track for about 1hr as it wends its way around the lake margin before bending sharp right to head uphill; the climb is short but steep. At the top of the rise meet a track and turn left, with a good view of the Monchique hills. As you descend ignore a track on the left, and continue downhill. At the bottom of the descent turn right onto a wide track that runs gradually uphill.

As the climb ends you come to a junction of tracks; turn right to follow a wide track uphill for a short distance before it levels out. Continue along this track, ignoring several others to left and right. After about 10min the track begins to head downhill, bending around to the right as it follows the hillside to reach a junction of tracks at the bottom of the descent. Turn right.

Follow the track as it descends to meet another, where you turn left. This is part of the outward route around the lake. Retrace your footsteps, and after 15min or so you should be back at the car park.

BARRAGEM DA BRAVURA

N

0   2 km

start/finish
of walk   dam

restaurant/café
Hansel and Gretel

Odaxiere

WALK 6
The National Forest of Barão

Distance	12.8km/8 miles
Time	4hrs
Grade	Moderately easy
Facilities	Barão S. Joaõ has several cafés.
Access	The church at Barão S. João. The village is located 10km west of Lagos. The easiest approach is from the A22, which you follow until it ends, close to the village of Bensafrim. From the roundabout marking the end of the A22 drive through Bensafrim towards Lagos. Immediately after leaving the village take the first road to the right and follow it for 5km to Barão S. João; the church is on the right. There are plenty of parking spaces in the village.

For most walkers the term 'forest' conjures up images of large areas of land under trees; here in the Algarve 'forest' refers to something far less pretentious. The 'Mata' or Forest of Barão refers to several hectares of land west of the village of Barão S. João, where attempts are being made to preserve the natural vegetation, now also home to a wind farm as Portugal seeks to find alternative sources of energy.

A circular walk through both woodland and open countryside, with panoramic views.

With your back to the church door walk up the main street. At the far end go right and then left, following the street until you meet a main road. Turn right and walk up the road through the village. Almost immediately there is a small road off to the left, which you ignore. Continue through the village, and on a sharp right bend turn left on another road.

Follow this road for about 6min when you will see a house on the left, '**Quinta Cileiro**'. Just past this the road/track forks; go right to head gently uphill. Two minutes later ignore a track to the right, and continue straight on. Follow this track along the contours of the hillside, ignoring various tracks and paths to left and right. Stay on the main

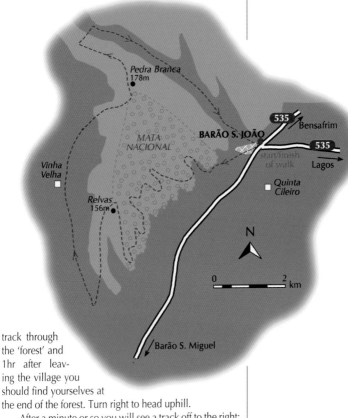

track through
the 'forest' and
1hr after leav-
ing the village you
should find yourselves at
the end of the forest. Turn right to head uphill.

After a minute or so you will see a track off to the right;
ignore this and continue uphill. The track levels out with
wonderful views to the left, then bends around to the right.
Here you will see a track going left, which you take, and
almost immediately you will find a large white-and-black
trig point (**Relvas**, 156m). Follow the track away from the
trig point; it soon forks and you go right to head downhill
and then climb up to meet another fork. This time go left;
the track follows the spine of a small ridge before descending to the valley below where you meet a wide track.

Turn right. Stay on this track for almost 2.4km (ignoring all turnings to left and right) and you will pass to the right of a farmstead 'Vinha Velha'. Stay on the track that heads away from the farm and its various outbuildings (now a Rudolph Steiner school). Ahead you can see the track heading uphill; at the top of the climb a track comes in from the right, but you go left. Almost immediately your track bends right to pass into the forest, but you keep straight ahead. After 5min cross over another road/track between concrete posts, heading towards two small concrete stumps. ◀

This brings you to the edge of an escarpment with panoramic views over the countryside all the way to the Monchique hills.

To your left you should be able to spot another trig point hidden amongst the bushes (**Pedra Branca**, 178m). Turn right to walk along the escarpment edge for about 2min before turning right along a much narrower track that heads into the woods. The track heads downhill through a mixture of woodland and bushes, and after about 15min you will reach the edge of the village and a surfaced road. Turn right. Immediately pass the village wash house on your right before the road forks; keep left. Walk up to the Rua das Parreiras where you turn right and then first left to retrace your footsteps back to the church.

Beyond Vinha Velha

WALK 7

The Coastal Path –
Porto do Mos (Lagos) to Salema

Distance	16.5km/10.25 miles
Time	5hrs
Grade	Moderate
Facilities	Cafés and restaurants in Praia da Luz, Burgau and Salema.
Access	Porto do Mós lies just to the west of the Ponta de Piedade close to Lagos.

Sadly this section of the coastal path has seen large-scale development, but the beauty of the cliffs and sea still remain and this coastal walk is very popular. If the whole walk is too long it can easily be joined in Praia da Luz or Burgau. The section from Burgau to Salema is by far the most interesting as you pass a 16th-century coastal fort, the remains of a Roman settlement, and the evocative wetland of Boca do Rio, home to many birds.

Start the walk by taking one of several paths heading up from the car park. When the path forks stay to the left, keeping parallel to the clifftop. Eventually you come to the '**Atalia**' (the large black-and-white obelisk). From here you have a choice: the most direct but steepest route is straight down from the obelisk, whereas there is a slightly less steep path just past the obelisk, partially obscured by trees. Once at the bottom follow the path leading away from the cliffs to reach a villa entrance on your right.

A clifftop walk that includes an old fort and Roman ruins.

Take the path to the left that leads downhill. Ignore any turnings right and soon you will reach the village of Luz. Continue straight on along the paved road where you turn left to walk past two café/bars and a large car park on your right. Bear slightly left to walk along a pedestrianised way above the beach. At the far end

57

the path bears right to head towards the church; once past this take the first road on your

left – the Rua da Calheta.

Continue straight along this road; eventually it gives way to an unpaved track, which you follow until you come to a small white building on your left. Bear left and follow the path along the cliffs. ◄ Follow the path parallel to the clifftops and eventually you will come to a small hill directly ahead. You can either take the path directly up and over this or, if you prefer, follow the small path that leads around the hill to the right; the paths rejoin on the other side. Now follow the clifftop path, ignoring any turnings off right, and eventually you will approach the village of **Burgau**. Turn right to walk down the street, bending left at the bottom into the centre. This is a working fishing village, and a good place for a lunch stop.

Once rested take either of the two main streets in Burgau that lead away from the sea to a crossroads at the top of the village, with a bus shelter across the road to your left. Turn left and take the road past the shelter signposted 'Quinta da Fortaleza'; this will take you out of the village.

At this point take care: you will see a very wide 'trench' on your left, and on the right there are three large holes that are partly obscured by foliage.

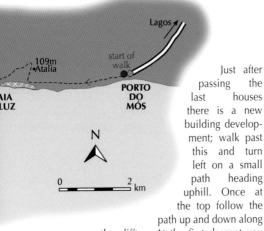

Just after passing the last houses there is a new building development; walk past this and turn left on a small path heading uphill. Once at the top follow the path up and down along the clifftop. At the first descent you should be able to see an old circular threshing circle in the field to your right. The main coastal path stays a short distance from the cliff edge but there are several offshoots to your left that will bring you closer; be careful if you take one of these. They are not to be recommended if you suffer from vertigo!

Eventually you ascend gently to a **red-and-white beacon**, marking the highest point along the coast (81m) and on a clear day offering a panoramic view. Behind there are views to Portimão and possibly Cape Carvoeiro; ahead the coastline extends all the way to Sagres. ▶ The path soon passes through a cutting and bends round to the left towards some ruined fishing huts. Turn right on a track on the bend and almost immediately look down on the beach of **Cabanhas Velhas**. Follow the track and eventually descend to a wide unsurfaced road. Directly opposite is your route, but first turn left to go down to the beach, which is well worth exploring.

Once refreshed go back up the road and take the first turning left on to a newly paved track that heads uphill, soon walking straight towards a large white house. Just before you reach it bear right to skirt around it through

As you begin to descend a track left leads above the Ponta da Almadena headland; take this short diversion for more wonderful views before continuing along the main path.

59

some pine trees. Then follow a path almost opposite, but slightly left, heading away from the house, follow this. Soon the ruins of an old building appear ahead, a 17th-century Spanish fort that was destroyed in the earthquake of 1755. Much of the original stonework remains, and the views from the outer walls are spectacular.

Behind the fort to the left follow a path that leads away from the building; it descends to a small stream. ◄ Once across walk through the parking area at the top of the beach towards some dilapidated huts (old storehouses for the fishermen's tuna nets; the large area behind these huts is the site of an old **Roman settlement**, yet to be excavated). In the cliffs to the right of the beach you can still clearly see the remains of an old Roman villa, sadly breaking up and being lost to the sea. Just off the coast here lies the wreck of the old French man-of-war galleon *L'Ocean*, which sank in 1759.

Take the path that heads uphill to the clifftop. Keep straight on, ignoring a wide unsurfaced road to your right, following the edge of the cliff. Right at the top the path heads inland away from the sea. Eventually you meet another track; bear left and follow the path downhill onto a surfaced road. Turn left and follow the road into the centre of **Salema** where you can either find a taxi or take the bus back to the start (the bus stop is just up the road to the right from the central square).

There are some stepping stones to help you cross, and at low tide it is possible to cross close to the beach (Boca do Rio).

Roman ruins in the cliffs, Boca do Rio

WALK 8

The Coastal Path – Salema to Sagres

Distance	17km/10.5 miles
Time	6hrs
Grade	Moderate
Facilities	Beach bars at Zavial, Ingrina and Martinhal beaches, offering food and drink. Wide variety of cafés and restaurants at Sagres.
Access	The car park by the beach in the centre of Salema. Salema lies 2km from the N125 between Lagos and Budens. Turn left at the traffic lights just past Budens; Salema is clearly signed. Alternatively take a bus from the bus station in Lagos.

This coastal section lies within the natural park, so at the moment it remains virtually unspoilt. It is fabulous walking, taking you down to beautiful beaches and then back up onto the clifftops. The coastal path out of Salema has been the subject of some development and further along it has badly deteriorated, so this route initially leads away from the cliffs to the village of Figueira before rejoining the coastal path near Zavial.

From the central car park in **Salema** take the road that passes the Hotel Salema; it bends to the left and then climbs steeply. At the top of the rise it levels out; follow it to a small village (**Figueira**) and meet a road. Turn left to walk through the village, and after crossing a small bridge take the first turning left, marked by several post-boxes.

Continue along the road, ignoring tracks to left and right. After about 10min the road starts to head downhill; turn left on a wide track. Follow the track to cross a stream on a small concrete bridge. The track then forks; take the right fork, heading directly uphill, passing a house off to the left. At the top you come to a junction of tracks where you turn left. The track again climbs, and you will see a house on the clifftop left.

This walk path takes you deep into the Cape St Vincent Natural Park.

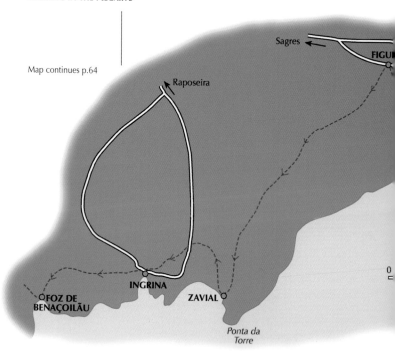

Map continues p.64

When the track forks bear right; the track becomes very wide as it meanders towards the headland of **Ponta da Torre**. (The path here can get a bit obscure – there are various tracks – but just aim for the headland, marked by a small mound.)

Once at the headland – and after a rest – take a short walk along the headland away from the sea and follow a path off to the left, descending the cliffs to **Zavial beach** below (a stick can be useful here as there is a fair amount of loose stone on the path). Walk across the sand to the beach bar and then walk through the car park to the road, where you turn left. Continue up the road, which rises then drops to reach another small beach and beach bar – **Ingrina**.

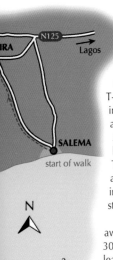

From Ingrina take the very wide track that passes behind the large abandoned building and climbs uphill parallel to the coast. Ignore all turnings left and right and continue to reach a T-junction. Turn right, ignore a turning almost immediately to the right, and follow the track. After about 5min you will see a beautiful sandy beach below (**Foz de Benaçoilãu**). Take care with your descent, for although the track widens it is steep in places and there can be loose stones underfoot.

Follow the wide track leading away from the beach; after about 300m you will see a path left which leads across a flat grassy area. Cross a small stream (dry for most of the year) using the stepping stones, then follow the track uphill. Once at the top meet a track on your right, but continue straight ahead. Not long after this there is a track off to the left, but continue straight on across the flat plain heading towards the **trig point** (55m), which you pass on your left. Meet another track coming in from the right, but ignore this and head towards an **old farm** and outbuildings.

Pass in front of the farm, ignore a small track right, and continue along the fairly wide sandy track until it forks. At the fork take the right branch; not long after the track forks again; take the right branch. Soon after the track forks once more, this time go *left* and you will soon head towards the sea. From a clearing just before the clifftop you will be able to see three small islands ahead; take a narrow footpath to the right. You should be able to spot this in the distance, following the clifftop. There are many offshoots at this point, so just stay close to the clifftop – but not too close to the edge!

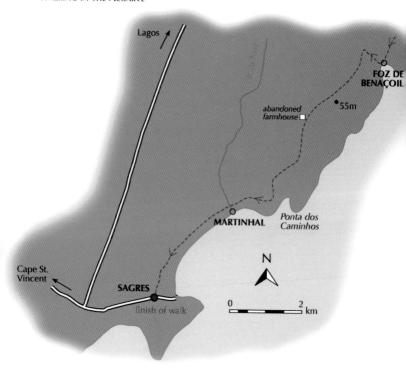

Eventually you will reach a small headland; take the narrow path that descends to the pebble beach below. Cross the beach. There is a steep but short climb, but this time do not go all the way up; bear left to follow a narrow path close to the cliff edge. When this path forks keep left again and you will soon reach the dunes above **Martinhal beach**. Walk along the beach, and at the far end follow a track into the village of **Sagres**.

When you meet a surfaced road turn right to walk along the main street; taxis and the bus stop are at the far end of the town.

WALK 9
The Slopes of Foia

Distance	8km/5 miles
Time	2.5hrs
Grade	Moderate; involves a climb of about 300m
Facilities	Wide variety of cafés and restaurants in Monchique; along the N266 many restaurants serving the local speciality 'chicken piri-piri' (barbecued chicken with a spicy sauce).
Access	The walk begins in the centre of Monchique town, reached by driving up the N266 from the coast. Once you have parked your car make your way back to the central square with the water wheel.

Foia (902m) is the highest mountain in the Algarve, but its summit has been spoilt by numerous telecommunication masts, souvenir shops and cafés – it is best avoided. The walk up to the top of Picota (Walk 11) will give you the same superb views, but without the crowds. However, there is still much to offer the walker here: ancient oak forests, abandoned terraced hillsides indicating former prosperity, and eucalyptus woods where the trees are grown for paper pulp and for use in the building industry.

A circular walk on the slopes of the highest mountain in the Algarve.

In the far corner of the town centre next to a small bus depot look for a shop with a yellow awning, the 'Garrafeira de Monchique'. Take the path to the left of this that heads uphill, then turn left (not sharp left) towards a large house; to the side of the house you will see donkey steps. Walk up the steps, which bend left to take you up to the next street.

An arrow on the wall opposite points left, but you go right and very soon turn left onto a cobbled road. Pass a garage on your right and almost immediately take a narrow path off to the right through the grass. The path heads up to a large white wall (the **cemetery** boundary) where you turn right to follow the wall uphill to meet a

Local houses in Monchique

wide track. Here you turn left, still following the wall, and continue on this track, passing some modern flats on your left, to meet another one where you turn right. Continue, ignoring a turning off left, to reach a fork. Bear left and almost immediately arrive at an old entrance marked by two cement posts.

Just to your right in front of the posts you will see a narrow path and an electricity pylon in the distance; turn right here and head for the pylon. By the pylon there is a small stone boundary mark with RM14 on it. Turn left to head uphill, following an old drystone wall. The path climbs over the rocks as it heads up to a wide glade where you can see some low-growing branches ahead. Pass under these to pick up the path again (the wall is always to your left).

The path climbs again over rocky outcrops before levelling off slightly, when you should see another large outcrop ahead. At this point the wall goes to the left. Pass to the right of the outcrop and ahead you will see a much clearer path leading up to an old track. Go right to follow the track uphill out of the woods to a car park on the right and a restaurant – the '**Jardim das Oliveiras**'. Beyond the car park are two small roads, take the left one, which will bring you up to a main road.

Cross the road; almost directly opposite follow a track heading uphill. The track soon forks; take the right-hand one to continue uphill through eucalyptus woods. There has been some logging here so part of the track may be obscured by branches, leaves and logs.

After a short climb ignore an overgrown track on the right, and continue up to the next very clear track off to the right. Turn right; many of the trees have been cut down so there are wonderful views over the foothills and down to the sea. This track leads to a surfaced road. Turn left.

Stay on the road as it bends right and then left before passing a ruin on the left, after which it bends again to the left. The road rises slightly before turning left, with great views to the east. Ignore an overgrown track off to the right. Less than 100m further on turn right on a good track that drops down into the woods. The track bends to the right, passing an old barn before descending to another old **abandoned farm building** on the right. Stay on this track.

The track drops down; ignore a track off to the right, then ascend to meet a wide track – turn right. The track descends again, bending right then left, and you will see several farmhouses scattered over the hillside. Ignore a track off to the right that leads to a farm; keep straight on. The track passes into the woods as it heads downhill; ignore a track off to the left heading uphill. Your track soon bends sharply down to the right, but at this point look for a much smaller track off to the left – turn left. This track is quite stony and has been scoured by rainwater, so take care. The track descends through the woods to meet a main road.

Cross the road and turn left. Walk along the road for a short distance to find a metal barrier on the bend. Pass throught the gap in the barrier to reach the path below. Go to the left on this path and follow it directly away from the road, slightly downhill. It is partly cobbled.

Local walkers

Descend between old walls. As you enter a small woodland turn right on a path that leads down to the old **Convento**. From here take the good track leading away from the building; it bends sharply to the right, and soon after there is a road to the left. Turn left and follow the signs through the old town of **Monchique** to the central square, via tiny streets.

Looking over the foothills of Foia

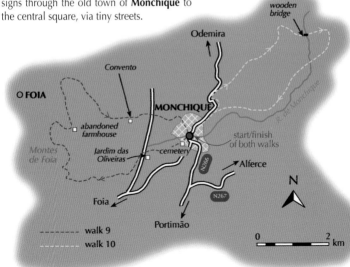

WALK 10
The Monchique River

Distance	7km/4.3 miles
Time	2hrs
Grade	Moderately easy
Facilities	See Walk 9.
Access	This walk also begins in Monchique central square (see Walk 9).

The rivers that have eroded through the Serra have left valleys rich in fertile alluvium. Here the locals grow a wide variety of fruit and vegetables in carefully tended plots and on terraced hillsides. Away from the terraces is mixed woodland, including many cork trees, which are harvested every nine years.

A circular walk through unspoilt mountain hamlets and countryside. This walk will show you a very different Monchique, and it can easily be combined with Walk 9, The Slopes of Foia. For map, see Walk 9.

Take the road leading away from the square; there is a sign for the Centro da Saude (this is the old Lisbon road). Follow the road for about 800m out of Monchique town. Pass some very large eucalyptus tree before bending sharply to the right, where the pavement ends. Continue along the road for another 50m to find a small cobbled track off to the right (just before the restaurant Bica Boa); turn right here.

After a short distance the cobbles give way to a normal dirt track that wends its way around the hillside. Follow this for about 15min to reach a small surfaced road; turn right. After about 200m ignore a road off to the right; at this junction cork is often piled up for collection. Soon after ignore further tracks off to the right. Stay on the surfaced road as it heads downhill, then bends sharp right before dropping down again. The road ends by a house on the right; keep straight ahead across a grassy area. The path can be quite obscure for a short distance here as it descends across some rocky outcrops to a small stream, which you cross on a **wooden bridge** provided by the council.

A newly stripped cork tree

Collecting cork

Once across the bridge turn left. Follow a narrow path up between the rocks to emerge opposite a house and surfaced road. Walk up the road until you come to a small road to the right; turn right. Almost immediately you will see a narrow path to follow off to the left (which can become overgrown). The vegetation will soon clear as you pass between small fields, before the path widens out and becomes cobbled. It leads uphill under a 19th-century aqueduct to meet a track at the top of the rise.

Cross straight over onto a wider track and follow this until it ends at the garden of an isolated house with maroon aluminium shutters. Just as the track bends slightly to lead into the garden take a path that continues straight ahead to pass directly in front of the house. This leads to another bridge; cross this then turn left, passing a smallholding on the left before the path gives way to a cement track. Black pigs can usually be seen here, reared for fine-flavoured ham. Continue along this track, passing between several houses, to meet a main road; turn right.

Walk along the road; it is normally very quiet, with little traffic. The road climbs up, passing an old wash house on the right, to meet the old Lisbon road. Turn left to walk back to the centre of **Monchique**.

WALK 11
Picota

Distance	14.5km/9 miles
Time	4hrs
Grade	Moderate, with a climb of 400m (mostly gradual)
Facilities	See Walk 9, The Slopes of Foia.
Access	The main square in the centre of Monchique (see Walk 9).

Picota is the twin of Foia, although it is a little lower (774m). The bonus for walkers is that it is not on the 'tourist route' so the summit offers a real haven of tranquillity, and on clear days spectacular views down to the coast as far as Cape St Vincent. Although partially planted with eucalyptus the slopes of Picota have a much more varied plant life than Foia and include the rare rhododendron (*Rhododendron ponticum* ssp *baeticum*).

Walk back along the Portimão road to the edge of town where you will see a road to the left to 'Alferce'. Turn left for about 500m, then turn right on a small road signed 'Picota'. Follow the road for about 800m; you will see a small surfaced road off to the right heading straight uphill. Before it there should be a blue arrow on the electricity pole indicating a right turn (ignore a sign for 'Picota' pointing straight down the road).

Walk up the road, and after about 20min ignore a small road off to the right; follow the main road around to the left to continue climbing. Shortly after the road bends sharply right by a house before straightening out; continue up the road and just as the road bends slightly left you will see a track going uphill in front of you – take this.

The track bends around to the right and then forks. Keep left to continue uphill; almost immediately the track forks again, and once more take the left fork that goes straight ahead. This track is a bit overgrown in parts as it passes

A wonderful circular walk to the top of the second-highest peak in the Algarve. There is a watch tower on the top of Picota, 'manned' 24 hours a day.

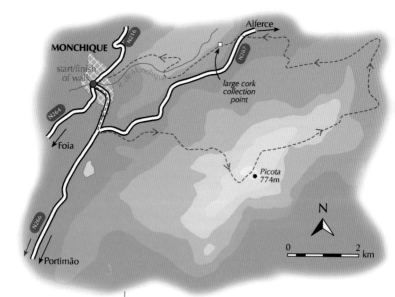

around the hillside through a eucalyptus plantation before entering woodland. Follow the track through the woods (much logging has taken place in 2011 and 2012 so there are considerably fewer mature trees standing) until at the top of the climb you emerge on to a small plateau; to your left you will see the large rocky outcrop of **Picota** (774m).

Take the path left to the edge of the rocks, which you must now climb up and left to reach the summit (there may be some orange dots on the rocks to help you but they are not really necessary). These rocks are never slippery so should not present too much of a problem.

Once at the summit cross over and descend on the far side to the small surfaced road visible below. Walk along the road, which then bends left to head quite steeply downhill. Follow the road down until you come to an electricity pole on the left. Almost opposite on the right is a track that you now take to pass through another eucalyptus plantation to meet another track; turn right.

Almost immediately you come to a crossroads of tracks where you turn left. The track passes through more eucalyptus before beginning to descend down the mountainside. After about 10min the track bends right to meet another wide track; turn left to continue downhill until you come to a small road at the bottom of the descent. Turn left.

Ignore a track off to the right and stay on the road as it passes around the hillside for about 40min when it reaches a wide surfaced road; turn right to head steeply downhill. At the first house on your right turn right on a small road that passes beside the house. Follow the road for about 200m, then turn left on a track heading downhill between fruit trees to emerge at a minor road; turn left.

Walk down the road for about 50m when you will see a track off to the right, passing a small house on your left. Turn right and follow the track through cork oaks before it bends left into a grassy clearing. The main track goes to the left, but look for a small footpath off to the right.

Wood working, Picota

Take the footpath to pass above a ruined house on your left. The path drops down over some rocks to take you away from the house before turning left to head downhill and becoming more of a track. Very soon you reach the main '**Alferce**' road; cross this and turn right. Stacks of eucalyptus lie along this road, ready for collection. Follow the road for about 100m, then turn left on a minor road. The road drops down and bends sharply left. Continue along the road, passing a large cork-collection point on your right (ignore a road off to the right) for about 15min. The people living in the scattered houses along this road still carry on their traditional way of life. You reach a road; turn right to walk downhill and cross the **Monchique river**.

As the road rises take a path off to the left behind the first house. The path soon widens and then forks as it approaches a house; take the right fork to walk above the house to meet a track Turn right and walk up the track for about 50m to meet a wide track; turn left. This leads to the hamlet of Cruz dos Madeiros. At the road turn left to walk up the hill to meet the old Lisbon road; turn left to return to the main square.

WALK 12

Ilha do Rosario

Distance	8km/5 miles; shorter walk (avoiding Ilha) 5.5km/3.4 miles
Time	2hrs; shorter walk 1.5hrs
Grade	Moderately easy for the full walk (with a climb of about 50m); the shorter walk is very easy.
Facilities	Café at the start offers meals at lunchtime.
Access	Drive over the bridge into Silves and turn left at the lights on the road for Portimão/Monchique. Follow the road straight over at the roundabout to leave Silves. After 5km you will see the Mira Rio café on the left; this is on a very sharp bend, so take care when turning into the café car park (where you can leave your car).

The 'Ilha' or island refers to a limestone hill that is bound by the Arade and Odelouca rivers and the Falacho stream. All three watercourses are tidal, and at low tide there are plenty of wading birds to be seen, particularly along the mudflats of the Arade. During spring the hillsides are awash with flowers including orchids, and when the nearby orange groves are in full blossom the scents can be quite overpowering.

Walk back along the road for about 20m before taking the track to the right. Ignore the track that goes up to the house; instead take a small footpath (it can get overgrown during spring) leading down to an irrigation channel which you cross on a small bridge. Turn left and walk beside the channel to reach a small surfaced road. Turn right.

A super walk through orange groves and along the banks of the Arade and Odelouca rivers.

Local produce

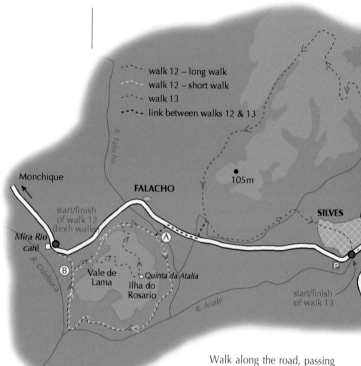

Walk along the road, passing over another irrigation channel before turning left on a small road heading uphill.

The road climbs gently before passing between houses into a hamlet. Continue through the hamlet until you see a road off to the right heading uphill. (*If you want to avoid the climb keep straight ahead on the road, which reduces to a track – this is the shorter version of the walk, which rejoins the main route below the hill.*)

Turn right along the road that ascends through the orange groves. Almost at the top you will see a track off to the left, bounded by two large concrete posts. Follow this track for about 10min to the abandoned **Quinta da Atalia** where the track goes left and then almost immediately forks – keep left. Follow the track as it brings you

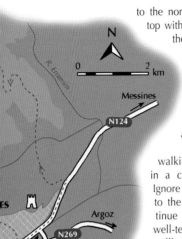

to the north side of the hilltop with superb views over the countryside before starting to descend.

At the bottom of the descent in front of a house go right; the track will lead you into another track.

You are now walking below the hill in a clockwise direction. Ignore the wide track off to the right (A) and continue straight on, passing well-tended fields and smallholdings on your right before passing under an aqueduct that carries water into the irrigation channels at certain times of year. The track brings you up to some houses where you will see an irrigation channel off to the left; take the path alongside this. Follow the channel until it passes under a very wide driveway that descends to a small watersports centre where at weekends you can sometimes get refreshments. From here there are very good views of Silves; it is also a good spot to watch the wading birds.

To continue the walk return to the channel, walking beside it with the **Arade river** on your left until you reach a house. The channel passes behind the house; keep walking beside it until it appears to bend around to the right. At this point turn left on a path that brings you to a small headland and the confluence of the Odelouca and Arade rivers with magnificent views – a superb picnic spot. The walk continues along the channel, with the **Odelouca river** on your left, to reach a surfaced road (B). Turn left and retrace your footsteps to the car.

WALK 13
North of Silves

Distance	12.4km/7.7 miles
Time	3hrs
Grade	Moderately easy
Facilities	Good selection of cafés and restaurants in Silves.
Access	The town of Silves is easily accessible from the A22 and the N125; when approaching the town turn left to cross the river and then left again at the traffic lights. Drive by the river and you will find a large car parking area on the left.

This half-day walk provides a complete contrast to the town of Silves. In summer the cool and quiet of the woods and countryside offer a welcome relief from the hustle and bustle of Silves with its many visitors. It can easily be combined with Walk 12, Ilha do Rosario.

A circular walk through the countryside and eucalyptus woods north of Silves town. For map, see walk 12.

Go to the road and turn right; walk up the road, passing the old Ponte Romana bridge. Continue to the roundabout, just beyond which you should be able to see a stone pillory. This has been built from 16th-century remains and is a symbol of municipal power; it is the only such structure in the whole of the Algarve. From the roundabout take the road that bears left to go past the cemetery. Immediately after the cemetery turn right (with the cemetery on your right). At its far end go left then immediately right, onto a small road with a stream on your right-hand side.

Continue along this, passing under a tall aqueduct and ignoring a road to the left. Almost immediately your road forks; take the left-hand one, going uphill. Continue upwards on this narrow road with a surface that has seen better days. Ignore turnings to left and right and eventually your road will fork; there is a small Algarve house on your right with a large plastic rubbish bin. The new surfaced road goes left but you go straight ahead; soon after your road becomes a track.

Keep straight on and soon head up to a col; to the right is a dilapidated house (goat farm). The track bears left to follow the hillside as it climbs; on the ridge you are faced with turnings to left and right. Go left and soon there is an excellent view south to the town of Silves. Your path goes around to the right; almost immediately turn right on a track to head downhill through eucalyptus woods.

Eventually you come to a junction of tracks; go right to follow a track out of the trees, following the contour of the hill before climbing up to an old ruin. Just before the ruin your track goes around to the left (ignore the track immediately left heading uphill); your path continues to follow the hillside, then proceeds downhill with a steep valley to your right.

Silves castle, seen from the walk

81

Stay on this path for quite some distance, passing a fenced-off area on the right, then the remains of some type of dump (right). Ignore a turning to the right arrowed with a broken white stone sign; about 500m further on your wide track bends to the left and you will see a track straight ahead, heading slightly downhill. Take this.

You may have to cross a small stream as you stay on this track, which soon bends to the right and emerges into more open countryside with grassy fields. Keep on the track, which then bears left; ignore another to the right. The track is flanked by olive groves and almond trees. Because of the heavy winter rains you may have to hop across the river several times as you continue. When orange groves appear on the right look out for a glimpse of a **trig point** (105m) up to your left; you are walking due south. Eventually the track bends sharply left and then right as it passes around the grounds of a long, low, white house with several dogs. It then rises slightly before becoming enclosed between old red sandstone walls.

Now descend towards a main road, but before reaching it pass a water irrigation channel where you turn left to walk on the path beside it (*if you want to link up with the Ilha do Rosario walk – see below – continue down to the main road*). Follow the channel until it meets a surfaced road where you turn right. This will bring you to another road; turn left. Pass the prison on your left and follow this road straight on into the centre of **Silves**.

Link to Walk 12

Walk down to the main road, cross it and turn right. Walk along the road for about 500m; turn left on a road signed 'Falacho'. Walk down to the junction and turn left again to reach A on Walk 12, Ilha do Rosario. Follow the notes for Walk 12, but at B turn right to return to A. Go back to the main road and retrace your steps to Silves to complete Walk 13.

WALK 14
Parra

Distance	13.4km/8.3 miles
Time	4hrs
Grade	Moderately easy, with a climb of about 100m towards the end.
Facilities	Two small cafés along the road from Silves to the start; closest restaurants are in Silves.
Access	Drive into Silves over the bridge and turn right at the lights, following the road along the river to the roundabout. Take the third exit, signposted 'Centro Saude'; almost immediately turn right at the corner of the cemetery, and right again at the T-junction. Continue along this road (to São Marcos da Serra) for 14.5km when you will see a wide parking area on the left-hand side of the road; just beyond there is a small sign on the left to Parra.

The Parra area has been designated national forest similar to that of Barão, but compared to the latter Parra is much less advanced – not helped but a devastating fire during the summer of 2003. However, this should not detract from the walking, which offers panoramic views northwards over the rolling hills and down to the Odelouca river.

From the parking area walk down the road and turn left along the wide track towards Parra. Follow this track for about 20min (ignoring any smaller ones to left and right) to reach a **restored house**, belonging to the forestry. Continue straight on, passing the house on your right; ahead you will see a **small hill** with an old building on top. At the base of this hill tracks lead to left and right; take the one to the right. Follow this all the way around the hill; it is little used (except by occasional forestry vehicles) but does offer panoramic views over the countryside and down to the Odelouca river whose banks are thickly vegetated with stands of alders and oaks. Beside the river there are some abandoned farmsteads.

A walk through countryside that sees very few visitors – wonderful.

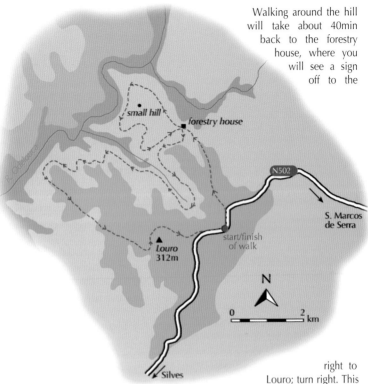

Walking around the hill will take about 40min back to the forestry house, where you will see a sign off to the

right to Louro; turn right. This small track is again little used and gives a feeling of complete isolation. Follow the track for about 90 minutes as it winds itself around the hillside before it ends sharply at an old bulldozed track that passes up and down the hillside.

Turn left and climb steeply up the track, ignoring other tracks to the left; the climb becomes more gradual before reaching a junction; turn left. Proceed straight ahead, passing tracks off to left and then right. Head towards a steep hill, keeping on the track, which passes to the right of it. Continue along the track through the eucalyptus woods; again you find yourselves climbing,

and once again you come to a junction, where you turn left.

Proceed straight along the track; a further climb up through the trees leads you out of the woods. Straight ahead you will see a hill and trig point: **Louro** (312m). Take the track that leads up the hill. You can either climb to the top and follow the track down the other side, or take the track left around the hill. Once around the hill meet the track that descends from the trig point; turn left. Continue straight along this track (ahead right you should see glimpses of the main road) and after about 10min reach the road; turn left. The road climbs for a short distance; just over the brow of the hill is the parking area where you started.

Abandoned farmstead close to the Odelouca river

85

WALK 15

The Coastal Path – Benagil to Vale de Engenho

Distance	10.4km/6.5 miles
Time	3hrs
Grade	Moderate
Facilities	Restaurants at the start in Benagil; beach bar at Albandeira.
Access	The easiest approach to Benagil is from the N125 near Lagoa. Driving eastwards from Lagoa, after 3km pass the International School on the left; take the first road to the right at the traffic lights (there should be a sign for Benagil). Follow this road and signs for about 5km when the road turns sharp left downhill (the O Litoral restaurant is at the top on the right; there are some parking spaces to the side).

This section of coastline is considered by many to be the most picturesque in the Algarve, and features on many postcards. A camera is a definite must as the multi-coloured cliffs are extremely photogenic, and in spring wild flowers abound. There are also some large blowholes which are quite spectacular; in recent years most of these have been fenced off so you will have no problem finding them. Some of the paths are rocky, and there are patches of loose stone, so if you have a walking pole take it with you. This walk commences at Benagil, a small traditional fishing village. Wander down to the beach to see the fishermen's colourful boats and old houses.

A clifftop walk that has some of the most spectacular coastal scenery in the whole of the Algarve.

Walk down the hill towards a restaurant on the left; by the side of the building you will see some old stone steps. Climb these to meet a track at the top; keep to the right along a path that for the most part follows the clifftops. Soon a slight descent leads past a very large blowhole to your left before climbing back up to overlook a beautiful beach, only accessible by boat. Look back to see several caves and other weird cliff formations.

Continue along the clifftop path until you reach a fairly steep descent into a gully; here there are choices to both left and right. To the left the way is, for the most part, marked by small orange dots on the rocks that lead you a little way inland. (If crossing this gulley by the 'inland' track, once you reach the path on the far side turn right to walk back towards the sea to rejoin the main walk at the cliff top; the views are worth the effort.) The choice to the right is perfectly possible, particularly if you have a pole.

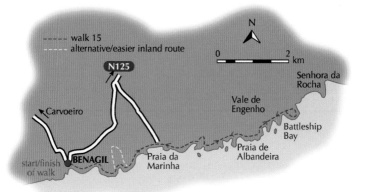

From here you have to climb up over the rocks to capture views eastwards, and then pick your way through the bushes following the path to the left, bringing you on to a headland with stunning coastline scenery. The path leads to a much wider track; follow this to the road, and turn right. Almost immediately you come to a large car park and some picnic tables (**Praia da Marinha**).

Walk through the car park; at the far end steps and then a concrete walk way lead above Marinha beach. ▷ To continue the walk go straight ahead and soon you are back on the clifftops. Follow the path for a good 5min; it narrows as it bends left away from the sea, descending to cross another gully. *At the bottom of the short descent a path immediately leads off to the right to a tiny beach, but*

To access the beach take the steps off to the right.

87

The coastline between Benagil and Praia da Marinha

the route follows the much wider track that climbs up the other side of the gully. Once at the top take a narrow path to the right that leads back to the clifftops.

Continue to follow the clifftop path; after another 10min note a spectacular arch to your right. ◄ From here there is a short descent to the beach and bar at **Albandeira** (with picnic tables for general use).

It is possible to walk over this arch (a good photo opportunity).

Walk behind the beach bar; climb up the steps and rocks to continue along the path close to the clifftops. The path becomes a much wider track which soon forks: go to the right and soon after enjoy views of a small rock stack out to sea known as **Battleship Rock**. ◄ The path leads down, then up and around to the right to a headland with great views eastwards to Armação de Pera and the beach of Gale. Here the path goes inland; over to the right you can see the small chapel of **Nossa Senhora da Rocha**.

To appreciate the reason for the name you need to look at the formation from the side!

From here a narrow path heads downhill to a very steep gully, but do not be tempted to take it; instead take a path to the left which leads back to the track on which you approached the headland. You now have retrace your footsteps to the start, but this coastline is so spectacular that the return route will offer even more photo opportunities.

WALK 16
Amorosa–Torre Hill Walk

Distance	11.5km/7.1 miles
Time	3.5hrs
Grade	Moderate
Facilities	Several cafés in Amorosa; restaurants on the main Silves–S. B. Messines road, and in both towns.
Access	Amorosa lies just north of the N124 Silves–Messines road. If coming from the coast travel up the IP1 (old Lisbon road) and take the exit for Messines/Silves. Follow the signs for Silves; the road to Amorosa is the first turn on the right after the Messines bypass. Drive down towards the village and park as soon as convenient.

This area is characterised by a fascinating and abrupt change of scenery as the underlying rock type changes from limestone to deep red sandstone and then to shale. This also involves a complete contrast in vegetation, from typical *barrocal* flora into orchards of citrus fruits and then to hillsides covered in gum cistus.

Walk down the road to the village and take the first road off to the left. Walk up the street; when it forks at the top go left and you will see a track to the left (the end of Walk 17, Amorosa–Zimbreira). Follow the surfaced road; it soon bends to the right. Almost immediately take a narrow walled road to the right (opposite the 'Casa Espinho'). At the end of the road turn left, then first right; on the corner is the sign for the 'Rua de Trabalhador'. This soon leads to a junction of roads; go left (there should be some rubbish bins on the left corner).

Walk along a surfaced and then unsurfaced track. Ignore turnings to left and right; keep straight ahead and soon ascend past some villas on the right; to the left is a large hill and trig point (**Gralheira**: 282m). Continue along the track, passing a new house on the left, with

A circular walk that crosses three different rock types with correspondingly different flora and fauna.

panoramic views ahead down the valley to Silves. Pass a house on the right, 'Vivenda Valverde'; stay on the track and eventually reach a junction of tracks. Take the narrow footpath opposite; this passes between fields, some of which have been abandoned.

This leads into the village of **Cortes**. Once through the arch turn right and walk between the houses. At the top the path bends left and passes some houses to reach the road, where you turn right. Ignore a road to the right and climb up to a café. Stay on the surfaced road through tiny hamlets – look out for threshing circles near some of the houses – with panoramic views left down to the coast, and after about 1km pass a new road off to the left. Continue straight on.

Look for a track off to the right just as the road begins to head uphill. Follow the track down and around the hillside, with good views across the valley to the Serra; it eventually levels out (ignore a track to the right) and continue to meet another track, where you turn right. This leads through citrus groves before bending left, then right, to reach a surfaced road.

Unspoilt countryside near Amorosa

Turn left; the road immediately forks. Take the right branch that descends to cross a small bridge; then turn right on to a track that heads uphill. Keep to the left when the track forks to continue up to the crest of the hill to meet another track; turn right.

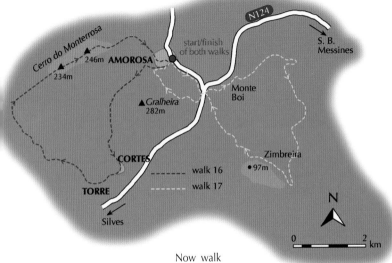

Now walk along the crest of a ridge, with several steep climbs and descents along the way; however, the views make up for any minor discomfort! At the top of the final climb follow the track downhill, slightly to the left and then to the right, to reach a wide track; turn right.

The track crosses deep red clay; most of the time the walking is easy, but after periods of heavy rainfall it can become both muddy and slippery. The track climbs gently; follow it all the way to the edge of the village of **Amorosa**, where you meet a minor road and turn left.

Follow the road straight down through the village until you meet a main road; turn right. Another 200m will bring you to the starting point.

WALK 17
Amorosa and Zimbreira

Distance	9km/5.6 miles
Time	2hrs
Grade	Easy
Facilities	See Walk 16.
Access	See Walk 16.

This is a short but interesting walk through unspoilt countryside near Messines. It can be combined with Walk 16, Amorosa–Torre, to make a full day's walk.

An interesting walk through the hamlets so typical of the Barrocal. For map, see Walk 16.

Walk back up the road to the main N124 and cross over to the small road opposite; take the first turning to the left, a small road that leads steadily uphill, passing the hamlet of **Monte Boi**. Once the road has passed the houses it bends around to the right; keep going until you see a small house on the right, with a track leading right just before it (about 30min from the start).

Turn right here and follow the track for about 150m to find another track to the left by a wall with a fence on top. Turn left here and follow the track gently downhill. Stay on this track as it winds through the countryside to meet a wide track; turn left and follow this one down to a small road.

Turn left and almost immediately right on a small road that heads gently upwards. The road soon bends around to the right; then take the first track off to the left. This leads to a house, which you pass on your right before turning right into a small hamlet. Walk through the hamlet and descend towards a surfaced road where you will see a track off to your left, heading downhill. Turn left and walk down to a crossroads of tracks; turn right to walk up through the hamlet of Zimbreira.

Follow the track around and below the hill of **Zimbreira** (97m). Meet one track coming in from the right, then turn right on another track; you are now walking with your back to the hill. Follow this track all the way to meet a surfaced road, then the main N124 where you turn left.

Walk for about 50m, then cross the road on to a small road signed Monte Novo. The road almost immediately bends left; follow it to meet another small road off to the right that heads uphill. Walk up the road to reach a large villa on the left; keep right on the road and follow it to the small hamlet of Monte Novo.

Walk between the houses; you will see a track off to the left opposite the 'Centro do Convivio do Monte Novo'. Turn left here and follow the track out of the hamlet, soon with a good view of Amorosa village below. The track descends past fields and smallholdings to the village, where you turn right. (*If linking up with Walk 16 turn left.*)

Follow the road around and then down to the right, passing the village school, to meet a main road; turn right for about 100m to the starting point.

The view across the valley to the Serra

93

WALK 18

Paderne Castle, Leitão and the Serra Grande

Distance	14.5km/9 miles, short walk (excluding Serra Grande) 11km/6.8 miles
Time	4hrs; short walk 3hrs
Grade	Moderately easy
Facilities	Excellent selection of cafés and restaurants in Paderne.
Access	For Paderne drive north on the IP1 and take the exit for Tunes; just after leaving the main road there is a right turn signposted 'Paderne'. Follow the road for about 5km to meet a main road; turn left and almost immediately right for Paderne. As you approach the village you will see a cemetery on the right, and just beyond a large parking area in front of a sports stadium.

Paderne is a picturesque village in a fertile cultivated valley surrounded by low-lying limestone hills 13km northeast of Albufeira. The old castle of Paderne lies 2km south of the village, perched high above a bend of the Quarteira river. The castle's origins are Moorish, although it was extensively rebuilt during the Middle Ages and a chapel erected on the site of a former mosque within the walls. Below is a beautiful stone bridge of Roman origin, partially rebuilt in the 19th century after it suffered damage during the 1755 earthquake. Leitão is a small hill (154m) situated between Paderne and the castle. The Serra Grande is a limestone ridge (rising to 227m) to the southeast of Paderne that offers wonderful views over the valley.

There are quite a few minor surfaced roads on this walk, but do not let this put you off – they are all quiet, with very little traffic.

LONG WALK

A walk along the Quarteira river, passing the old Roman bridge ▶

Walk back to the **cemetery**; take the road to the left running uphill beside it. Follow the road around to left and then right, passing the local school on the right. Follow this narrow road for about 1km before it becomes a track and leads down to a minor road. Turn right, and walk down the road until you see a wide track to the left signed 'Castelo'; turn left here. Follow this track between fields of fruit, olive and almond trees, and soon the castle comes into view.

The track passes under the motorway; turn left to follow another wide track uphill. At the top of the rise find another track to the right – *this leads to the castle* – but to continue the walk keep straight ahead. Stay on this track, passing several turnings to the left before heading downhill to the river where you turn right, passing several old ruined buildings (including a well-preserved beehive oven) as you approach the bridge.

Pass the bridge on your left and follow a narrow path above the river with the castle high above on your right. The path follows the bend of the river before leading down to a much wider path; at this point

and then a Moorish castle before returning through tiny hamlets with wonderful views.

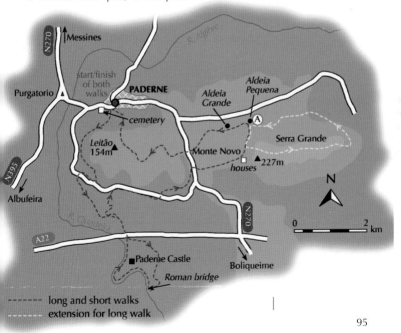

————— long and short walks
————— extension for long walk

Old 'beehive' oven near the bridge over the Quarteira river

there is a renovated olive mill across the river, now a family home. Walk along the track under the motorway and retrace your steps back to the minor road.

Once at the road turn right, and walk uphill until you see another minor road off to the right; turn right. Continue along the road, passing some cottages before the road bends sharply to the left; keep on the road until you come to another small group of houses and a road to the left. Turn left here for about 100m when you will see a track off to the right passing in front of two houses; turn right here.

Follow this track through the countryside until it brings you to another one; turn left and almost immediately right, passing in front of another country house. Continue on this track all the way to the main road. Cross the road and turn left; after 20m you will see a track off to your right that runs beside a house with a fenced garden.

Walk straight up the track, ignoring others to left and right. Continue straight on, climbing gradually to meet a surfaced road. Turn right. Continue straight along the road, and after passing houses on the left ▶ and right, proceed straight ahead uphill. The track soon levels out and follows the north side of the **Serra Grande** ridge, offering superb views over the countryside towards Rocha de Pena and Alte.

The shorter walk turns left here: see below.

At the end of the ridge the track appears to be slightly obscured by bushes, but proceed straight ahead and almost immediately the bushes give way to lower-growing thyme and lavender. The track leads down the far side of the ridge; about halfway along, when the track goes sharply to the right, turn left on another. This track is very little used and can be overgrown in places. Follow it around the hillside before it descends to meet another; turn left here (look out for a well-built drystone wall to the left).

This very clear track leads up to meet another, with a well-renovated house on your right; turn right to follow the track/road around and through a small hamlet (Casas de Pouço). Follow the road out of the hamlet, and after about 500m descend to meet a main road. Just before the road turn left on another minor road. Follow this up to and through

The Roman bridge over the Quarteira river

the small hamlet of **Aldeia Pequena** (A). Just after leaving the hamlet the road bends around to the right; on the bend keep straight ahead on a track between the fields.

This track leads to the small village of **Aldeia Grande**. At the junction go right (there is a tiny shop with a red postbox on the wall on the corner) and immediately left. Continue straight on through the village, ignoring a small road off to the left; stay on the road as it rises slightly to a junction where you turn left, then descend between the houses to the main road.

Cross the road, and take the track directly opposite that leads uphill. At the top of the climb meet a minor road; turn right and follow the road down to meet another. Turn left for about 800m to find a sign right to '**Moinho do Leitão**'. Walk up this small road to the top of the rise where it meets a track. *Go left to reach the hilltop.* The walk continues to the right. Follow the track down the hillside and around to the left before meeting a road. Turn right and retrace your steps to the start of the walk.

SHORT WALK

Turn left by the side of the house on the left onto a small path that leads downhill. This leads directly into the hamlet of **Aldeia Pequena** where you turn left (A), rejoining the route of the long walk.

WALK 19
Esteval dos Mouros

Distance	12km/7.5 miles
Time	3hrs
Grade	Moderately easy, with a gentle climb of 150m
Facilities	Small café in Esteval dos Mouros is not always open; good selection of cafés and restaurants in Alte (north), Paderne (south).
Access	Drive into the village of Paderne and take the road to Lentiscais. As you enter the village turn right towards Esteval dos Mouros. Follow the road for about 4km to reach a junction; turn right; about 50m along on your left is the abandoned primary school where you can park.

The old village of Esteval dos Mouros nestles between the hills of Cabeça Aguda and Rocha Amarela in the heart of the Barrocal. Much of this area is reinventing itself as farmers move towards growing citrus and other fruits on a more economic scale, aided by grants from the EEC. Nevertheless, this area has experienced a dramatic decline in population, particularly during the 70s when people moved to the coast in search of a better way of life. Many houses and villages were abandoned, one good example being Rocha Amarela, located on the side of the hill that shares its name. The village remains almost intact, and even though the houses are in ruins they offer a unique glimpse into a way of life that is rapidly disappearing.

Walk down the road into the village (the houses are scattered along it for almost 2km). After less than 10min pass through a narrow section with a high old wall on the left and the walls of a house on the right. After this the village opens up again; you will see some houses up to the left away from the road. Opposite the road leading to these houses turn right on a track that heads down into a large plantation of fruit trees.

A walk to the abandoned village of Rocha Amarela.

Follow the track to the end of the trees; stay on it as it bends left to pass behind them. Ignore several tracks off to left and right and keep ahead until you meet a good wide track; turn right. Walk along the track; ignore another to the right soon after. Stay on the track and about 15min later you will pass a very large pile of rocks on the right, and just beyond it a large agricultural store. At this point turn left on another track.

The track soon bears around to the left before heading up towards a modern rounded storehouse and junction of tracks; keep straight ahead, passing the storehouse on your left. Continue along the track, passing a similar storehouse on the right. After about 3min turn left on another track.

After about 100m the track bends to the right, then winds between fields. Ignore a track to the left as your track begins to climb gently up the hillside to reach a small surfaced road. Turn left.

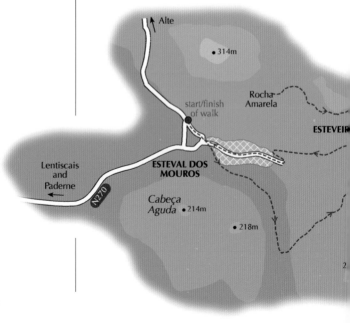

Walk up the road; as you approach a hamlet of houses turn right on a wide track. The track passes through scrub before bending around to the left as it climbs gently up the hillside, then levels out. Pass an abandoned farmhouse on the left; after about 10min arrive at the abandoned village of **Rocha Amarela**. From here on a clear day there are views right down to the coast. Once you have finished looking around the village you must retrace you steps back to the road, where you turn right.

Typical housing with blue 'platibandas' in Esteveira

The road ends at the far end of the hamlet of **Esteveira** – with typical Algarve houses decorated with traditional blue *platibandas* around windows and doors – and becomes a track that heads downhill. Follow it down to meet a track where you turn right to continue descending all the way to **Esteval dos Mouros**. As you reach the edge of the village turn left; soon meet a concrete road where you turn right. This will bring you into the centre of the village where you will see a small bar just to the right of the main road. Turn right at the road to walk back through the village to your car.

255m•

m
Cabeça Gorda

101

WALK 20
Rocha da Pena

Distance	8km/5 miles
Time	2.5hrs
Grade	Moderate, with a climb of 150m
Facilities	Café at start/finish; restaurants in Benafim and Salir.
Access	Take the N124 from Alte towards Salir. After passing through Benafim drive past the village of Pena; as you begin to approach Salir turn left at Taipa towards Alcaria. After passing through Alcaria turn left on the road signed for 'Rocha da Pena' and follow it for about 2km to the Fonte dos Amadoas; café on the right.

Rocha da Pena is an imposing limestone escarpment that became a protected site in 1991 in order to protect the diversity of flora and fauna that live here. More than 390 different species of plants have been identified, filling the landscape with both scent and colour. The area is also home to more than 122 different species of birds, including jays and buzzards, the migratory Bonelli's eagle, grey heron and redwing, and in summer the European bee-eater and the cuckoo. Rabbits, wild boar, foxes, genets and the Egyptian mongoose are also resident, together with two species of bats: the Schreiber's bat and the lesser mouse-eared bat, which are on the verge of extinction.

A walk up to and along a limestone escarpment that is also a classified site.

The track up to Rocha de Pena runs up by the side of the café, quite steeply at first, but becoming more gradual as you approach a small wooded area. In spring there is a profusion of the beautiful wild peony here. The track soon bends to the right to pass directly below the steep scarp face. After about 20min of climbing the track reaches a clearing which marks the top of the hill. Go right along a track that takes you to the northern edge of the rock, with superb views northwards over the countryside.

Return to the clearing and take the path directly ahead (to your left is the track you arrived on). Follow it until you reach a very large stone bank (Neolithic in origin). Pick your way over the bank, following the path, which leads to a clearing; from here follow a track uphill.

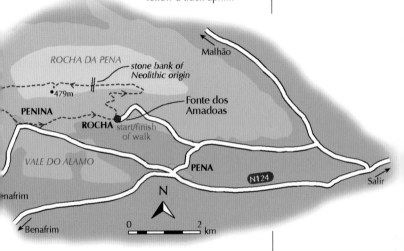

After the gentle climb the path levels out and then begins to descend; at this point turn left on a path that brings you to the **trig point** (479m) where there are stunning views southwards to the sea. Retrace your steps down to the path and turn left to continue. The track now descends the west side of the rock and can be quite stony in places, so care is needed.

The track leads into the village of **Penina**; turn right to head down into the village centre and the road, where you turn left. Follow the road; just after leaving the village turn left on a wide track. Follow this as it bends right to pass below the scarp face to return to **Fonte dos Amadaos** in about 20min.

WALK 21
Pé do Coelho

Distance	8km/5 miles
Time	2.5hrs
Grade	Moderate, with a climb and descent of 260m. The descent is on a stony track which is quite steep in places; a pole would be useful.
Facilities	Café at Malhão serves light meals.
Access	Follow the directions for Rocha da Pena, but instead of turning off in Alcaria continue along the road for 7.5km. When you come to the hamlet of Pé do Coelho, turn left off the main road and park the car.

Behind the limestone escarpment of Rocha da Pena the geology changes to schists and shales, creating a very different landscape. In the fertile valleys lie the remnants of small plots once irrigated with water drawn up from old wells (*noras*); today large new fields have been created and water is lifted by pumps. The walk leads along the beautiful Arade river valley before climbing up to the top of the Cerro do Malhão.

A walk along the Arade river then up to the Cerro do Malhão (537m), one of the highest points in the area. The Cerro was originally a windmill and is now a Buddhist monastery, unique in Portugal.

(*With your back to the main road note a track off to the right that heads uphill: this is your return route.*)

Follow the narrow surfaced road through the hamlet. As you pass the final house the road becomes a track leading down to the river, which you cross. Continue along this track through the valley for about 4km (it crosses the river several times on the way) to enter the hamlet of **Corte Buxo**, passing some isolated houses before the hamlet proper. On the edge of the hamlet you will see a small house on the left with a small stone water tank; opposite is a garage and a track running uphill. Turn right to begin climbing. After passing a small orchard on your right you should see a small reservoir down in the valley.

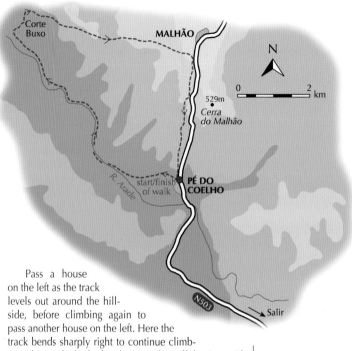

Pass a house on the left as the track levels out around the hillside, before climbing again to pass another house on the left. Here the track bends sharply right to continue climbing. This track climbs for almost 2.5km (all the time with panoramic views over to the right to Rocha da Pena and Rocha dos Soidos) to reach a surfaced road and the edge of the village of **Malhão**; turn right.

Walk down the road for about 200m to find a café on the left; just past the café the road forks. Almost opposite that fork turn right on a small track heading downhill below the surfaced road. The track leads down and around the hillside before descending quite steeply down to the edge of **Pé do Coelho** and your car.

WALK 22
The Hamlets Around Salir

Distance	15.2km/9.4 miles
Time	4.5hrs
Grade	Easy
Facilities	Cafés and restaurants in Salir; café in Ponte de Salir.
Access	If approaching from Loulé, drive around Salir following the signs for Alte. This will bring you down to the N124 junction; turn left and take the first right for the 'Estadio'. The sports stadium is just along on the right, and there is good shaded parking for cars. If coming from the Alte direction the left turn for the 'Estadio' is about 1km after the turn to Alcaria and Rocha da Pena.

Surrounding the large village of Salir are a series of small hamlets famed for their traditional dry orchards of carob, almond and olive. Like much of the rural Algarve this once thriving area has succumbed to a serious decline in population as the young move away, leaving behind a struggling elderly community. Many of the once prosperous orchards have now been invaded by the mastic tree, wild olives and kermes oak, and some of the hamlets have almost been abandoned. The area also has the greatest concentration of wells in the whole Algarve, giving some indication of how prosperous it once was. Now, sadly, very little is grown and the water wheels above the wells have been left to rust.

A walk that offers a real insight into the lives and livelihoods of the country people.

Walk up the road for about 200m, passing a house on your right; just beyond the house turn right onto a track. About 5min later reach a small agricultural building on your right and a track; turn right to walk in an easterly direction.

Continue along this track, ignoring any others to left or right, until you come to a surfaced road. Turn right; take the first left to head uphill on a concrete track. At the top of the climb the concrete gives way to a sandy track, which almost immediately forks. Take the left branch. The track

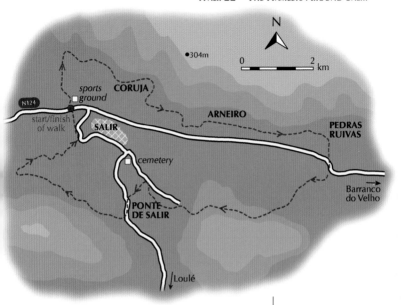

passes a small watering tap as it bends around to the right to lead between houses into the hamlet of **Coruja**.

Stay on the small road as it passes the houses before reaching a wide junction. Go right, and follow the road up to a fork. Go right and head slightly downhill, passing a small track and stone cross on the right; just beyond these turn left onto a track. Soon pass a house on the left and continue straight on for 10–15min when the track bends sharp right and heads slightly downhill towards the main road. At the bottom of this minor descent take the narrow road off to the left.

This road leads up to a junction; turn left towards the hamlet of **Arneiro**. As you enter the hamlet take the first road off to the right. This soon bends around to the left where it forks – keep right. Follow this very minor road for about 5–10min when it will bend sharply to the right; keep straight ahead on a red sandy track (there may be a sign to 'Quinta da Alforrabeira').

Looking towards Rocha da Pena

Just over 5min later the track rises to meet another. Turn left to head downhill, passing some large cork trees (cork was removed from these in 2004). When you meet a track go right, and right again at the next junction to come down to the main Salir–Barranco do Velho road. Cross straight over on to a wide sandy track.

Follow the track for 800m to pass Quinta da Cazenove on your right. The track begins to head downhill towards a river; about halfway down turn right onto another. Follow this through grassy fields and it will soon bring you to an old stone wall. Turn left at the wall and take the narrow path down to the stream which you cross; climb up the bank on the far side. Turn right, and follow the path above the stream into a field with large olive trees at its margins (in spring the field will probably be planted with maize). Walk to the far end of the field, then turn left to follow the field edge to the end where you will see a track; follow this.

The track heads uphill through light woodland to reach a very wide track; turn right. Walk along the track for about 500m when it will bend sharp left; keep straight on along a smaller track. Ignore a track soon after on the right and 5min later reach a minor road; turn left to drop down to another road. Cross directly over onto a minor road.

Follow the road around to the right. It ends by some houses; turn right on a track that passes in front of one house before dropping down to meet another; go right to head up to a surfaced road. Turn left.

Walk up the road. Pass a small watering area with a tap on the left, then take the track left just after it (just beyond on the main road is a sign 'Fonte de Ouro'). Almost immediately the track forks; go right to walk between old stone walls before rising up to meet a track where you go right. Follow the track up to another surfaced road where you turn left and walk up to a small cemetery on your left. Just beyond the cemetery take a track to the left.

Stay on the track that passes behind the cemetery and turn right by the cemetery flower 'dump'. This soon declines into a well-trodden footpath that leads across grassy fields up to a wall where you turn left. Follow the path around the wall down to the main Loulé–Salir road. Turn left.

Follow the road down to **Ponte de Salir** and cross the bridge. About 20m beyond the bridge turn right on a track. (*There is a café in the village: just continue up the main road for about 200m.*)

An abandoned nora (well) close to Salir

The outskirts of Salir

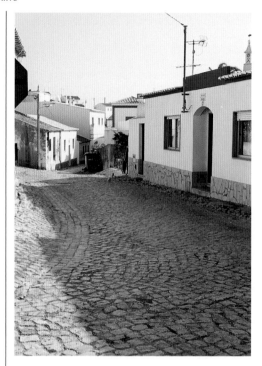

Continue along the track for about 1.5km when you come to a small hamlet and a surfaced road. Turn right and at the next junction go right again; then take the first small road off to the left. Pass the Casa da Fonte on your right as you follow the road past many abandoned wells before crossing a small bridge. Follow the road around and uphill. At the top of the rise go left, passing a small metalworks on the left before meeting a track where you again go left.

Almost immediately the track bends sharp left; turn right on a track on the bend and head gently downhill before crossing a minor stream and rising to a main Alte–Salir road. Cross directly over onto the minor road and follow it back to your car.

WALK 23

Querença and the Fonte de Benemola

Distance	15.9km/9.9 miles (excluding the Fonte); long walk 21.4km/13.3 miles
Time	4hrs; long walk 6hrs
Grade	Moderately easy
Facilities	Café and restaurant in the main square in Querença.
Access	Querença lies just off the N396 Loulé-to-Barranco Velho road; approximately 10km from Loulé turn left (the village is well signed), then almost immediately left again to drive up to the square where there is parking.

The village of Querença sits perched on a small hilltop surrounded by beautiful countryside. The focal point of the village is its square, with the delightful parish church of Nossa Senhora da Assunçao on one side and a small manor house on the other. The church dates from 1745 and was extensively restored on 1966, but its origins are much older. The impressive Manueline doorway dates from 1460–1520 and the beautiful interior depicts grapes, olives, figs and doves, all in gold leaf. The manor house is home to the offices of the parish council. Within the square there is a large cross of uncertain date.

The Fonte de Benemola was declared a classified site in 1991 to protect its unique and varied flora and fauna and outstanding natural beauty. The river cuts through both limestone and shale, and along the river banks giant reeds are grown for basket making.

SHORT WALK

With your back to the church door walk directly across the square, passing the old stone cross and the offices of the 'Junta da Freguesia' on your left. Take the road heading downhill away from the church. Drop down to a small chapel, and take the small road to the left that continues descending.

A great walk through beautiful countryside and river valleys to this classified site, famous for its flora and fauna.

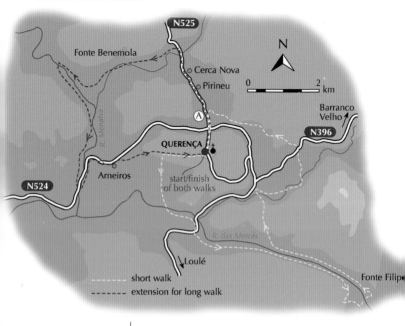

Pass a small road to the right and continue until you come to another turning to the right, the 'Travessa do Pombal', where you will see a blue and white spring outlet with a tap. Opposite this there is a turn to the left signed 'calcada medieval' this is an old cobbled path – turn here. The path again descends, the cobbles becoming a track just before meeting a small concrete road. Turn right to follow the road downhill to meet another road.

Continue straight on across a bridge. The road bends to the left before turning sharp right; on this bend turn left on a small concrete road that heads uphill. Soon the road levels out as it follows the valley high above the river. Continue to meet a main road; turn right.

Walk up the road for about 150m when the road bends sharply right. Turn left on this bend on a track that descends to another surfaced track, where you turn left.

Stay on this for about 2.4km, en route passing the restaurant 'Moinho Ti Casinha' on your left. Your path parallels the valley side until it comes to a clearing and forks; turn right onto a small road that soon leads to a wider road; turn left.

Follow the road to a wide clearing where there is a well on the right; turn left to cross a bridge, again staying on the road. About 100m after the bridge the road bends to the right, and just before the sign for 'Almarjão' take a track off to the left that leads down to a clearing. After the clearing the track turns sharply left; continue along it (now on the other side of the river valley). After a short time you approach a small farm building on the left and ignore two tracks that lead uphill; your track turns to the left to continue along the valley side.

This is now a wide good track that runs parallel to the river; you follow it all the way for about 15min when it then begins to climb up taking you away from the valley. Another 10min and you come to a clear T-junction where you turn left to head downhill to cross a small bridge.

Once across the bridge turn almost immediately right onto another track. Continue on this to reach a small stream which you cross (via stepping stones). Once across continue along the track which meets another wider one; turn left downhill. Again you must cross the stream; there is no bridge, but plenty of stones downstream to the left.

Looking northwards from Querença

After the stream the track begins to climb quite steeply up to a small road; turn right to walk down to a main road. Cross directly over onto a small road – the Caminho da Corte Garcia. Pass between two houses before the road bends left, then right, before straightening out. Continue along on a minor concrete road, passing some houses on the left, then follow the road through countryside up to a house where it bend sharply right. Follow the road and head up to a small hamlet before meeting another road; turn right.

Almost immediately turn left on the road to **Borno**. This narrow road winds between the houses of the hamlet to reach a wider road; to return to **Querença** turn left (A). Follow the road up to a junction, and continue straight on to meet a main road. Cross directly over; follow the road uphill back to the church. As you walk up the hill take time to look back over the countryside.

LONG WALK

To extend the 'short' walk and continue on to Fonte Benemola turn right at A and follow the road down to meet another road. Turn right and walk along the road, passing through the hamlet of **Pirineu** into the hamlet of **Cerca Nova**. The road climbs; after about 150m turn left to '**Fonte Benemola**'.

The track leads down along the hillside to meet another wide track; turn right. Pass an old farmhouse on the right before coming to the Fonte; continue to a small picnic area. Just after this you should be able to cross the river on stepping stones. Once across the river turn left onto a track and continue along it, ignoring any turns to left or right.

The track follows the hillsides before dropping down to meet a surfaced road; turn left to cross a bridge. Turn left and follow the road for about 500m until you see a minor road off to the right to **Arneiros**. Turn right and follow the road downhill before it bends sharply right. Just after the bend turn left on a track/minor road. This heads uphill for a good kilometre back to **Querença**.

Querença church

WALK 24

Estoi

Distance	11.5km/7.1 miles
Time	2.5hrs
Grade	Moderately easy
Facilities	Cafés and restaurants in Estoi.
Access	Drive along the A22 towards Spain and come off at the São Bras/Estoi exit (next one after the Faro exit). Follow the signs for Estoi; the road leads into the centre, opposite a large church. You should be able to find parking in the square to the left.

The small town of Estoi has two sights of historical interest, almost on each other's doorstep, yet almost 2000 years apart in age. Close to the main square is the Palacio de Estoi (also known as Palacio do Visconde), a pink rococo pastiche unique to the region; it was the brainchild of a local nobleman who died soon after work started. Another local man bought the palace and spent huge sums of money on what was to be his new home. The building was completed in 1909 but abandoned 80 years later, and then with the passing of time it fell into disrepair. It has now been converted into a luxury hotel. The gardens used to be open to the public but sadly no more. On the outskirts of Estoi lies the Roman complex of Milreu, dating from the 1st–2nd century AD. The remains of a luxurious villa, complete with baths and temple, can also be visited (Tuesday to Saturday). This walk passes both sites.

A walk passing the Roman ruins of Milreu and the Palacio de Estoi.

With your back to the church walk down the main road on which you arrived, passing the Roman ruins on your right. Cross over the road at the bottom and walk straight up to the main **Faro/São Bras road**; cross diagonally right to a small surfaced road. Walk up this, keeping straight on when the surface gives way to a track. The track rises to a T-junction; turn right to cross over the A22 motorway. Continue to meet another T-junction; turn right.

Continue along this wide track, passing a quarry on the left before climbing gradually to meet a small surfaced road. Turn right to cross a bridge and meet a main road. Turn left and walk along the road for under 5mins before taking a small surfaced road off to the right. The road climbs quite steeply; take time to stop and look at the view behind you. At the top of the climb the surfaced road becomes a track; follow this until it bends sharply down to the right. On the bend turn left on another overgrown track that runs parallel to the crest of the hill.

Enjoy views first right and then left before passing the ruins of **two windmills** on your right (partly obscured by trees and bushes) and then a villa. The track becomes surfaced as it descends to meet a small road; turn right. Continue straight ahead (ignore a road off to the right) and soon the surface gives

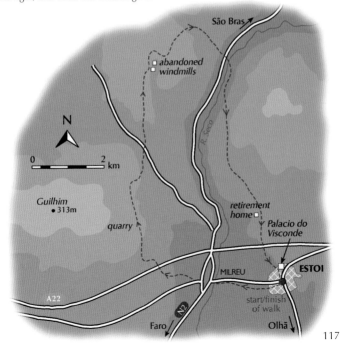

117

way to a track that passes between fields. At a fork in front of a villa keep right.

The track is poor as it leads downhill to a T-junction with a large house ahead; turn left. Almost immediately by an entrance to another house turn right on a path running between drystone walls. The path is overgrown, but persevere and after 5min or so you will reach a small house; go left to bypass it. To the rear of the house take a track left, heading steeply downhill.

The track bends sharply right; ignore the next track to the left, and follow the track around the bend right. Soon you will meet a track; go left to continue downhill to a main road. Cross directly over the road to the small surfaced road opposite which leads down to a bridge above the **Rio Seco**.

After crossing the bridge the track bends slightly to the right to run parallel to the river as it climbs up gradually. Continue straight ahead. ignoring tracks to left and right, until you come to a prominent fork; go left. Soon there are views of Estoi ahead; on your right pass a large new building (a **retirement home**). The track crosses over the A22 before coming to a junction of tracks; go straight ahead.

The grounds of the Palacio de Estoi are on your left. The track leads beneath a bridge linking the palace to its formal gardens before passing a wash house and fountain on your left. Take the first narrow street to the right; this leads to another street where you again go right to walk down to the main square and church.

Time for a chat, Estoi

THE SERRA DO CALDEIRÃO

This extremely beautiful area remains totally unspoilt. The Serra do Caldeirão mountain range straddles the northeast Algarve and southeast Alentejo, and much of it lies well away from the usual tourist routes. Like many rural areas in Portugal it is experiencing an exodus of its younger people who leave to look for better employment opportunities along the coast or abroad.

The IN LOCO ('On the Spot') Association was formed in 1988 with the twin aim of promoting community development and promoting the area to the outside world. As part of the initiative they have recently opened up a series of nine walks of varying lengths that show the best features of the area. The walks are centred around three small villages – Caixas Baixas, Feiteira and Mealha – and all are well signposted and clearly marked, so there is no need to describe the routes in detail here. *The following text is a translation of the walks leaflet that is available from the IN LOCO office.* Unfortunately the walks are neither well publicised nor well known, but do not let that put you off – all nine routes are beautiful and well worth the effort.

Cafés and restaurants can be found at Cachopo, which is central to all three villages.

CASAS BAIXAS, WALKS 25–27

From Cachopo take the main road south towards Tavira. About 1km from the town turn left on a small road (the sign is not clear until you have turned); follow the road for 3km to the edge of the village where you will see large information board on the left. It is best to park here. To find the start of all three walks, walk down the road and then bear left towards Alcarias Baixas; you will see the starting points arrowed on the right.

WALK 25

PR1, D. Quixote Walk
(16.9km/10.5km; 6–7hrs)

A walk to the River Odeleite, returning through totally unspoilt countryside.

This walk leads between hills of holm oak and carefully tended fields down to the River Odeleite, where you can see abandoned watermills.

Casas Baixas–Amoreira (4.6km/2.9 miles)
The first stage of the walk explores the tiny villages of **Casas Baixas** and **Alcarias Baixas** with their typical rural houses before heading north passing farms of cork oaks and hillsides planted with pine trees to **Amoreira**.

Cerro do Bicudo–Barranco da Junqueira (5km/3.1 miles)
After crossing the surfaced road the walk continues in the direction of the trig point on top of Cerro do Bicudo. The track is shaded with a wide variety of trees – including arbutus, pine, holm oak and the mastic bush – as it wends its way down to the **Odeleite river**.

Grainho–Moinho Velho (5.3km/3.3 miles)
The track climbs up from the river to the hilltop of **Grainho** where you have panoramic views over the countryside; here you can appreciate the importance of agriculture to the economy of this area. From here the track goes northwards passing old windmills and a countryside that is a mosaic of small fields and whitewashed houses.

Passa Frio–Casas Baixas (2km/1.2 miles)
The gentle track wends its way back to **Casas Baixas** flanked on either side by streams and springs.

WALK 26

PR2, Fonte Da Zorra Walk
(5km/3.1 miles; 2hrs)

This short walk, where you can see a variety of stone-built houses so typical of the region, is a must for lovers of rural architecture. Beehives will be seen on the hillsides, producing some of the finest honey in the Algarve. Beeswax is used for top-grade polish and ecclesiastical candles.

An easy introduction to this remote area.

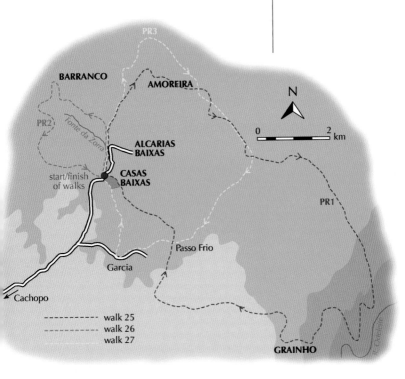

*On the way to
Fonte da Zorra*

Casas Baixas–Barranco da Fonte da Zorra (2.2km/1.4 miles)

The first part of the walk is the same as PR1 and takes you to **Alcarias Baixas** with its typical stone houses. Continuing north from here the track is one that is used frequently by the local people to get to and from their fields and small vegetable gardens. In winter the track can become flooded after heavy rain, so care is needed.

Barranco do Porco–Casas Biaxas
(2.8km/1.7 miles)
The path gently winds through fields and gardens to return you to **Casas Baixas**.

WALK 27
PR3, Montes Serranos Walk
(9km/5.6 miles; 3hrs)

This walk takes you eastwards from Casas Baixas, crossing the 'mountains' of Garcia, Passafrio, Amoreira and Alcarias Baixas; along the way there are wonderful panoramas over the countryside and Serra.

A walk that takes you up and over four surrounding hilltops, with panoramic views.

Casas Baixas–Amoreira (3.5km/2.2 miles)
Once again the first part of the walk is the same as PR1 and PR2, taking you to **Alcarias Baixas**, but then it continues in a northerly direction to the River Foupanilha. From here the track turns southeastwards to the hilltop village of **Amoreira**.

Amoreira–Casas Baixas (5.5km/3.4 miles)
The trail takes you up into the hills through beautiful countryside where along the way there are plenty of opportunities to stop and just wonder. As you approach **Casas Baixas** ruined windmills remind you of times gone by.

FEITEIRA, WALKS 28–30

The village of Feiteira lies almost halfway between Barranco do Velho and Cachopo on the N124. If approaching from Barranco do Velho the large information board detailing the starting points for the three walks is on the right just before you enter the village. The hill tops surrounding Feiteira are now home to a wind farm. Although this does not interfere with the walks some walkers may find their presence off-putting.

WALK 28

PR4, Cerros da Sobro Walk
(14.3km/8.8 miles; 6hrs)

A challenging walk through the countryside, with some steep climbs of more than 240m.

This walk takes you southwest from Feiteira down to the River Odeleite.

Feiteira–Castelão (4km/2.5 miles)

This part of the walk takes you from Feiteira to Castelão; along the way you soon begin to appreciate the importance of the cork oak to the local economy. After the climb to **Castelão** you are rewarded with superb views.

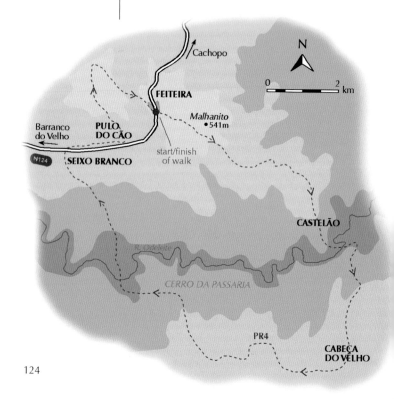

Cabeça do Velho (4.7km/2.9 miles)
The track descends to the **River Odeleite** where you can picnic on the banks of the river while watching the birds and enjoying the fragrance of wild herbs, especially in spring. Once refreshed climb up to **Cabeça do Velho** for more panoramic vistas.

Cerro da Passaria–Seixo Branco (3.6km/2.2 miles)
The path once again descends to the **River Odeleite** before ascending to **Seixo Branco**. The countryside here is full of the arbutus bush whose berries are used to produce the local 'firewater' *medronho*; in autumn the scarlet berries bring a bright splash of colour to the landscape.

Pulo do Cão–Feiteira (2km/1.2 miles)
The track takes you to the N124 where you turn right and walk along the road for about 1km to the **Pulo do Cão** crossroads where the trail goes off to the left. This part of the walk is shaded by cork trees which are grown on north-facing terraces.

View over the Serra from Malhanito

WALK 29

PR5, The Reserve
(6km/3.7 miles; 2hrs)

A circular walk through a nature reserve rich in birds and plants.

This short circular walk leads through a reserve with a wonderful variety of birds and plant life. To find the start walk through Feiteira in the direction of Cachopo. Just after the road bends to the right you will see a small single-storey house on the left; the trail is arrowed off to the left immediately beside it.

Feiteira–Cerro Alto (2.5km/1.6 miles)
The countryside along this part of the walk is a mixture of eucalyptus, cork oak, pine and typical Mediterranean scrub; in winter the path is liable to flooding. The trail takes you to a spring where delicious cool mountain water can be tasted and water bottles refilled.

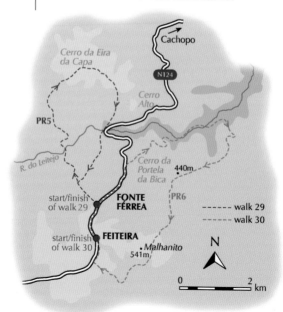

126

Cerro da Eira da Capa–Feiteira (3.5km/2.2 miles)
On this half of the walk you come to one of the highest points on the route where there is a magnificent view northwestwards. This terrain of deep valleys and high mountains offers an excellent refuge to many raptors, including the short-toed eagle and the buzzard.

Harvest time in Feiteira

WALK 30
PR6, Malhanito
(9km/5.6 miles; 3hrs)

The walk takes you to the top of Malhanito (541m), where there is a 360° panorama of the Serra, then drops down to the cool of the River Leitejo which offers a welcome relief for your efforts. The actual start of the walk is 1km to the north of Feiteira along the N124 in the direction of Cachopo.

Walk from the top of Malhanito down to the River Leitejo.

Feiteira–Fonte Ferrea (2km/1.2 miles)
The trail is rich with a wide variety of plants and takes you to one of the most famous springs in the area where many local families come to fill up their water bottles.

127

Cerro da Portela da Bica (3km/1.9 miles)

The track ascends slowly up to **Cerro da Portela** (440m), allowing you plenty of time to look at the local birds which abound here.

Malhanito–Feieiras (4km/2.5 miles)

The climb continues to the top of **Malhanito** on a good track before arriving at Castelão where you meet a surfaced road. From here back to **Feiteiras** is not only easy walking but is singularly beautiful, rural simplicity at its best.

MEALHA, WALKS 31–33

Thanks to an EC grant the village of Mealha is now linked to the rest of the Algarve by a surfaced road. From Cachopo take the road towards Martinlongo, and after about 300m turn left as signed for Mealha. Drive along the road for 8km to reach the edge of the village. A large information board about the walks (Walks 31–33) will be in front of you, and the local primary school on the right.

WALK 31

PR7, Vale das Hortas

(13.5km/8.4 miles; 5hrs)

This route follows the River da Corte, and offers a great insight into the mountain people and their way of life

This walk takes you westwards from Mealha, crossing the Corte João Marques and the Valley of Hortas, following the River da Corte. The hillsides have been planted with holm oak and pine, while in the valleys apple and olive orchards can be found.

Mealha–Barragem da Mealha (3.5km/2.2 miles)

The first part of the walk is along narrow stone pathways that cross the countryside taking you down to the small valley where a dam has

Ameixial

been built to create a reservoir; the water is vital in summer to irrigate the surrounding fields.

Vale das Hortas (3km/1.9 miles)

After crossing the **da Corte river** on a cement walkway the track becomes quite overgrown; do take care. The track takes you to another small bridge which, once crossed, offers you a chance to visit the **Pisão mill** – a watermill that is in a very good state of repair.

Corte João Marques (7km/4.3 miles)

After returning to the track you now head in an easterly direction following the **da Corte river** for a while and there is further evidence of other watermills, now just piles of stones. After leaving the valley the track climbs gently, winding around the fields to take you past one of the most interesting features of the area – round stone houses with conical thatched roofs.

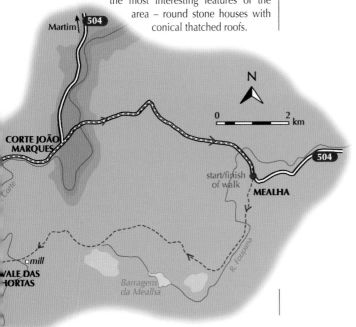

WALK 32

PR8, Masmorra
(6km/3.7 miles; 2hrs)

Explore the remains of a prehistoric burial chamber.

This walk takes you to Masmorra (350m) where you can see small villages scattered over the countryside and can really appreciate the tough, lonely existence that the people through the centuries have had to endure here. Close by are the stones of a burial chamber dating back to about 2500BC.

Mealha–Ribeirinha (3.5km/2.2 miles)
The walk begins by taking you down through the village to the local stream where abandoned hay lofts and animal pens allow you to appreciate that this area was once a thriving rural community. The rolling countryside is

A local farmer from Mealha

extremely pretty and in spring it is full of the heady scents of rosemary, lavender and thyme.

Masmorra–Mealha (2.5km/1.6 miles)
From the river the track climbs gradually to **Masmorra** where to the northeast you can see the hills of Barrada, Mestras and Martinlongo, to the north the windmill of Pereirão, and to the northwest the village of Ameixal. On the top of Masmorra you can clearly see the large stones that made up the burial chamber. The track descends back to the river before a short climb to **Mealha**.

WALK 33

PR9, The Burial Chamber of Pedras Altas

(10km/6.5 miles; 3hrs)

This walk takes you past old watermills, through beautiful countryside to another prehistoric burial chamber; it incorporates the best elements of the previous two walks.

Mealha–Antas das Pedras Altas (3.5km/2.2 miles)
The walk first takes you past the typical round stone houses that are in various states of repair before passing

Visit a prehistoric site, passing examples of the area's famous thatched circular houses on the way.

through farmland to the burial chamber of **Pedras Altas**.

Barragem–Ribeira da Foupana (3km/1.9 miles)

From Pedras Brancas the track passes between fields of lupins, cereals and market garden produce, then through woods of eucalyptus as it descends to the **Foupana river**. The river offers you the opportunity to stop and appreciate the area; to the east are the remains of an old watermill (Azenha da Valeira), to the west abandoned fruit trees and old wells.

Azenha da Valeira–Mealha (3.5km/2.2 miles)

You return along the same track before turning right to walk through rolling countryside where you might see bee eaters, stonechats and azure-winged magpies, as this area is home to a wide variety of birds.

The famous round houses of Mealha

WALK 34

The Mata Nacional da Conceição
and the Ribeira da Zambujosa

Distance	13.4km/8.3 miles; short walk 8.5km/5.3 miles
Time	3hrs; short walk 2hrs
Grade	Moderately easy. A river has to be crossed seven times; if there has been little rain this is not a problem; otherwise you must use stepping stones, or wade across.
Facilities	Cafés and restaurants in Tavira.
Access	Drive to Tavira, then take the N125 eastwards towards Vila Real de San Antonio; look for the large 'Eurohotel' on the left-hand side. Turn left 300m beyond the hotel where there is a sign for the 'Mata Nacional da Conceição'. The road soon bends to the right to cross a bridge; after 3km come to a junction and turn left. Follow the road which passes under the motorway; almost immediately you will see a parking area on the left, together with a map of the forest. Perched on a hillock to the left is the Casa do Guarda Florestal, a white building hidden among trees.

The Mata Nacional (national forest) north of Tavira is a relatively small area of woodland that has been dissected by the A22 motorway; do not let this put you off, for this is a wonderful walk. Beyond the forest to the north the landscape is dotted with tiny hamlets that see very few visitors; to the south are rolling green hills and farmsteads. Because the area is so unspoilt there is every chance of seeing a wide variety of animals and birds. During my research I was lucky enough to spot an otter, inadvertently disturbed a buzzard perched in the branches of a tree where I was having a water break, watched a hawk swoop on its prey and heard the familiar sounds of the woodpecker.

LONG WALK

Walk down the track between the Casa do Guarda Florestal and the parking area; soon after ignore a track to the right. Continue straight down, pass an old well on

A great walk through woodland and unspoilt counrtyside – the river has to be forded seven times!

133

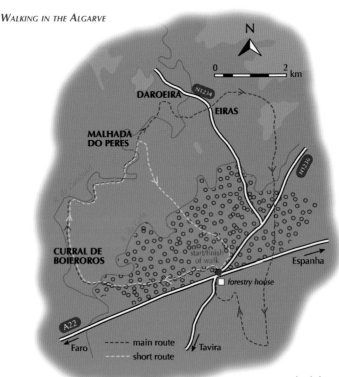

the left and
follow the track as
it bends left, passing two tracks to the
right that lead up to a house. Your track leads around
the hillside and gradually downhill to cross a small stone
bridge; ignore a track almost immediately to the left. The
track climbs gently; pass two more tracks to the left before
descending to cross a river bed. Here you leave the forest
and the countryside begins to open out.

Climb up towards the hamlet of **Curral de Boieroros**,
passing a small house on the left, and just before it a wide
track to the right. By the side of a smallholding ignore a
track to the left which leads into the hamlet; continue
straight on for about 200m when you will see a track to the
left dropping to cross the river. Keep straight ahead, with

the river on your left; this will bring you down to a wide river bed where on the far bank you can see a track – but don't be fooled! Cross the river bed towards the track, but before reaching the far bank turn right and walk along the river. Almost immediately you should see a track ahead of you across the river on the right, which you should take.

The track now follows the Ribeira da Zambujal, dropping down on several occasions to cross it. Stay on the main track and after 15min or so the hamlet of **Malhada do Peres** will appear ahead. The track drops once more to cross the river before heading up to the hamlet where you come to a junction of tracks; the full walk continues straight ahead in the direction of Eiras and Daroeira. *The short walk turns right here.* Once again walk beside the river before the track drops to cross it. ▶ Almost immediately after the crossing the track forks; keep right towards Daroeira.

Climb gently and you can see the river down to the right. At the next fork keep left towards the hamlet of **Daroeira**. As you approach the hamlet ignore a road to the left that leads up to the houses, and continue straight ahead, dropping to cross the river once more. Approximately 200m after the crossing ignore a track to the right; your track bends to the left and heads up towards some houses in the hamlet of **Eiras**.

Come out at a small surfaced road. Cross straight over onto another track in the direction of Caseta and Castelos. When the track forks go right towards Castelos. Ignore a track right and stay on the main track as it climbs up. Almost at the top of the rise the track forks: go right. The track climbs slightly to pass the hamlet of Castelos on the left. ▶ Soon head towards a small cluster of houses and it would appear that the track ends; continue straight ahead, passing to the left of the houses, and almost immediately the track opens out again. Start to head downhill to cross a river (Ribeira da Gafa). The track bends to the right; almost immediately turn left on a much smaller track through the trees.

Follow the track for about 5min to emerge onto a surfaced road and a road junction. Cross over, turn right

Here the track has been concreted and there are stepping stones at either side.

You are now walking along a ridge with wonderful views both left and right.

135

and then turn left on to a wide track. Proceed straight ahead, ignoring tracks to left and right, and shortly cross over the motorway on a modern bridge. You now head due south, and the countryside changes to rolling green hills. The track is very, very straight before leading up to a ridge and a junction of roads; turn right.

Walk along the road for about 500m. Turn right on a track opposite a two-storey house on the left. The track soon drops slightly to cross a small stream and appears to be heading directly to a farmstead. Just before the farm it forks; go left onto a small stony track that leads around the hillside. You are now passing between fields; the track becomes less clear and the stones give way to grass. At the next farmstead go left and almost immediately right to pass in front of the farm to your right and come to a small road.

Turn right: walk for 300m back to the car park.

SHORT WALK

Follow the main walk to **Malhada do Peres** to the junction of tracks and turn right. The track leads gently uphill, with a panoramic view to the right. Ignore tracks to left and right as you begin to descend to cross a small river. The track heads uphill before levelling off; stay on this track until you meet a surfaced road. Turn left; walk for 300m back to the car park.

A typical farmstead near Daroeira

136

APPENDIX 1

Language

Anyone familiar with other European languages such as French, Italian – and especially Spanish – will be able to comprehend some written Portuguese. However, speaking the language and understanding what you hear is another matter entirely, particularly in the Algarve where there is a very strong regional accent.

Many vowels are nasalised, and most 's' sounds are 'shushed', giving a very different quality to the language which takes some getting used to. The nasalised vowel sounds are indicated by a tilde as in *não*, the word for 'no'. This is pronounced somewhere between 'no' and 'now' when the nostrils are pinched together. Words ending in 'n' or 'm' are pronounced as though there is a 'g' on the end. For example *bom dia* ('good morning') sounds a bit like 'bong dia', without the 'g' being pronounced. An 's' at the beginning of the a word is pronounced as in 'soft', but elsewhere as 'sh'. *Sou ingles* ('I am English') is pronounced 'soh inglaysh'.

All this sounds very difficult – and it is! – but it is also well worth learning to speak a few words. In hotels and restaurants close to the tourist areas most of the staff speak English, but in the countryside only Portuguese is used. The people are very friendly and nothing can be more rewarding than to see their smile of delight when you try and speak a few words in their language.

USEFUL WORDS AND PHRASES

Ten essentials

English	*Portuguese*
Yes/No	*sim/não*
Hello	*olá*
Good morning	*bom dia*
Good afternoon	*boa tarde*
Good night	*boa noite*
Please	*faz favor*
Thank you	*obrigado (for a man)*
	obrigada (for a woman)
Thank you very much	*muito obrigado/a*

| I'm sorry | *desculpe-me* |
| I don't understand | *não entendo* |

More basic

Do you speak English?	*fala ingles?*
Please write it down	*escreva, faz favor*
Can you help me?	*Pode ajudar-me?*
I don't know	*não sei*
Where is -	*onde é*
The footpath to…	*a caminho para*
The road to…	*a estrada para*
The bus stop	*a paragem*
Here	*aqui or cá*
There	*ali or lá*
To the left	*a esquerda*
To the right	*a direita*
Straight ahead	*sempre em frente*
Behind	*atras*
Above	*em cima*
Below	*em baixo*
First/second/third	*primeiro/segundo/terceiro*
Is it far?	*é longe?*
I'd like	*queria*
We'd like	*queriamos*
What's that?	*o que é isso*
How much is it?	*quanto custa*
Do you have?	*tem*
That's fine	*está bem*
Where are the toilets?	*onde ficar os lavabos?*

Spring flowers near Sagres (Walk 8)

APPENDIX 2
Route Table

Walk no/name	Distance	Time	Grade
1 Esteveira	2.5km	1hr	easy
2 Pontal, Carrapateira and Vilharina			
full walk	16km	5hrs	moderate
short walk	6km	2hrs	easy
3 The West Coast			
full walk	19km	6hrs	mod/easy
short walk	4km	1.5hrs	easy
4 Bensafrim	10.4km	3hrs	mod/easy
5 Barragem da Bravura	10km	3hrs	mod/easy
6 The National Forest of Barao	12.8km	4hrs	mod/easy
7 The Coastal Path – Porto do Mos to Salema	16.5km	5hrs	moderate
8 The Coastal Path – Salema to Sagres	17km	6hrs	moderate
9 The Slopes of Foia	8km	2.5hrs	moderate
10 The Monchique River	7km	2hrs	mod easy
11 Picota	14.5km	4hrs	moderate
12 Ilha do Rosario			
full walk	8km	2hrs	mod/easy
short walk	5km	1.5hrs	easy
13 North of Silves	12.4km	3hrs	mod easy
14 Parra	13.4km	4hrs	mod easy
15 The Coastal Path – Benagil to Vale de Engenho	10.4km	3hrs	moderate

Walk no/name	Distance	Time	Grade
16 Amorosa–Torre Hill Walk	11.5km	3.5hrs	moderate
17 Amorosa and Zimbreira	9km	2hrs	easy
18 Paderne			
full walk	14.5km	4hrs	mod/easy
short walk	11km	3hrs	mod/easy
19 Esteval dos Mouros	12km	3hrs	mod/easy
20 Rocha de Pena	8km	2.5hrs	moderate
21 Pé do Coelho	8km	2.5hrs	moderate
22 The Hamlets around Salir	15.2km	4.5hrs	easy
23 Querença and the Fonte de Benemola			
full walk	21.4km	6hrs	mod/easy
short walk	15.9km	4hrs	mod/easy
24 Estoi	11.5km	2.5hrs	mod/easy
25 Casas Baixas: D. Quixote	17km	6–7hrs	moderate
26 Casas Baixas: Fonte da Zorra	5km	2hrs	easy
27 Casas Baixas: Montes Serranos	9km	3hrs	moderate
28 Feiteira: Cerros de Sobro	14.3km	6hrs	mod/diff
29 Feiteira: The Reserve	6km	2hrs	mod/easy
30 Feiteira: Malhanito	9km	3hrs	moderate
31 Mealha: Vale das Hortas	13.5km	5hrs	mod/easy
32 Mealha: Masmorra	6km	2hrs	mod/easy
33 Mealha: The Burial Chamber of Pedras Altas	8.5km	3hrs	mod/easy
34 The Mata Nacional da Conceiçao and the Ribeira da Zambujosa			
full walk	13.4km	3hrs	mod/easy
short walk	8.5km	2hrs	mod/easy

APPENDIX 3
Contact Details

British Consulate (Portimao)	282 490 750

Tourist Information Offices

Faro
Av. Da republica, 18   289 800 400
Airport   289 818 582

Albufeira
Rua 5 De Outubro   289 585 279

Aljezur
Largo do Mercado   282 998 229

Alvor
R. Dr Afonso Costa, 51   282 457 540

Armacao de Pera
Avenida Marginal   282 312 145

Carvoeiro
Largo da Praia   282 357 728

Lagos
Rua Vasco de Gama   282 763 031

Monchique
Largo dos Choroes   282 911 189

Portimao
Opposite the football stadium   282 416 556

Sagres
Rua Comandante Matoso   282 624 873

Silves
Rua 25 de Abril   282 442 255

Tavira
Praca da Republica   281 322 511

Airlines

BA	www.ba.com
TAP	www.tap-airportugal.co.uk
EasyJet	www.easyjet.com
Monarch	www.flymonarch.com

Bus Travel
www.eva-bus.net

National Railways
www.cp.pt

General Websites
(including details on property rentals and car hire)
www.portugal-info.net
www.algarve-info.net
www.portugalresident.com
www.algarve-information.com
www.algarvenet.com
www.algarve-web.com

Walking
www.portugalwalks.com

Maps
1:25,000 maps can be obtained from:
Instituto Geografico do Exercito
Av. Dr Alfredo Bensaude
1849–014 Lisbon
Tel: +351 218 505 300
Fax: +351 218 532 119
www.igeoe.pt

Stanfords
Customer Services Departmentt
12–14 Long Acre
London WC2E 9LP
sales@stanfords.co.uk
www.stanfords.co.uk

CICERONE EUROPEAN WALKING GUIDES

For full information on all our
British and international guides,
books and eBooks, visit our
website: **www.cicerone.co.uk**.

Walking – Trekking – Mountaineering – Climbing – Cycling

Over 40 years, Cicerone have built up an outstanding collection of 300 guides, inspiring all sorts of amazing adventures.

Every guide comes from extensive exploration and research by our expert authors, all with a passion for their subjects. They are frequently praised, endorsed and used by clubs, instructors and outdoor organisations.

All our titles can now be bought as **e-books** and many as iPad and Kindle files and we will continue to make all our guides available for these and many other devices.

Our website shows any **new information** we've received since a book was published. Please do let us know if you find anything has changed, so that we can pass on the latest details. On our **website** you'll also find some great ideas and lots of information, including sample chapters, contents lists, reviews, articles and a photo gallery.

It's easy to keep in touch with what's going on at Cicerone, by getting our monthly **free e-newsletter**, which is full of offers, competitions, up-to-date information and topical articles. You can subscribe on our home page and also follow us on **Facebook** and **Twitter**, as well as our **blog**.

Cicerone – the very best guides for exploring the world.

CICERONE

2 Police Square Milnthorpe Cumbria LA7 7PY
Tel: 015395 62069 info@cicerone.co.uk
www.cicerone.co.uk